3·26·76

The Christian Peace Shelf

No. 7

NO KING BUT CAESAR?

A Catholic Lawyer Looks at Christian Violence

By William R. Durland

The Christian Peace Shelf

The Christian Peace Shelf is a series of books and pamphlets devoted to the promotion of Christian peace principles and their applications. The editor, appointed by the Mennonite Central Committee Peace Section, and an editorial board, from the Brethren in Christ, General Conference Mennonite Church, Mennonite Brethren Church, and Mennonite Church, represent the historic concern for peace within these brotherhoods.

1. *Nevertheless* by John H. Yoder, 1971. The varieties of Christian pacifism.

2. *Coals of Fire* by Elizabeth Hershberger Bauman, 1954. Stories for young readers of men and women who practiced returning good for evil.

3. *The Original Revolution* by John H. Yoder, 1972. Essays on Christian pacifism.

4. *The Christian and Warfare* by Jacob J. Enz, 1972. The roots of pacifism in the Old Testament.

5. *What Belongs to Caesar?* by Donald D. Kaufman, 1969. A discussion on the Christian's response to the payment of war taxes.

6. *Jesus and the Nonviolent Revolution* by André Trocmé, 1973. A response to the anguish of our generation.

7. *No King but Caesar?* by William R. Durland, 1975. A Catholic lawyer looks at Christian violence.

NO KING BUT CAESAR?

No King But Caesar?

A Catholic Lawyer Looks at Christian Violence

William R. Durland

Introduction by Richard T. McSorley, S.J.

HERALD PRESS
Scottdale, Pennsylvania
Kitchener, Ontario
1975

Library of Congress Cataloging in Publication Data

Durland, William R 1931-
No king but Caesar?

(The Christian peace shelf; no. 7)
Bibliography: p.
Includes index.
1. Violence — Moral and religious aspects.
I. Title 261.8 74-30093
BT736.15.D87
ISBN 0-8361-1757-3

Library of Congress Catalog Card Number: 74-30093
International Standard Book Number: 0-8361-1757-3
Printed in the United States of America
Design by Alice B. Shetler

To the Holy Spirit

In Memory of
The Early Christians

Cain set on his brother Abel and killed him.

Genesis 4:8.

If a man injures his neighbor, what he has done must be done to him: broken limb for broken limb, eye for eye, tooth for tooth.

Leviticus 24:19, 20.

You have learned how it was said: Eye for eye and tooth for tooth. But I say this to you: offer the wicked man no resistance.

Matthew 5:38, 39.

Contents

Editor's Foreword

The Christian Peace Shelf was established a number of years ago to publish both classic and current studies in Christian pacifism. We are pleased to be able to add to the shelf this readable volume *No King but Caesar?* by William R. Durland.

The strength of this book is the wrestling of a serious disciple with the violence of the church through the centuries. This investigation by a sensitive conscience is a stimulating reminder how the Holy Spirit continues to speak through events, in this case both the war in Vietnam and antiwar demonstrations. This work also illustrates a wholesome way of rediscovering forgotten and distorted truths. The admonition of the apostle to search the Scriptures is well illustrated. The uses of tradition and history are amply justified.

There are numerous varieties of pacifisms. Each one's insight enriches the others by expanding the vision or complementing inadequate understandings. Old pacifists and established pacifisms need the enthusiasm and critical sensitivities of the new. New pacifists and innovative pacifisms need the memories of suffering servanthood of the old. This volume by a Roman Catholic demonstrates the fresh zeal of a newly found faith. The argument with Christian violence keeps alive the awareness that peace and nonviolence are continuing agenda items for fraternal dialogue.

This is not intended to be a comprehensive study — yet this Catholic pacifist's look at Christian violence should help readers of all persuasions sense anew the dilemmas of Christian faithfulness.

John A. Lapp
Editor, The Christian Peace Shelf
Chairman, Mennonite Central Commitee Peace Section

Introduction

Since the time of Augustine, Christians generally have gone along with every war their particular Caesar called for. As a result of subservience to Caesar we entered the nuclear age with a theology which was developed for the bow and arrow age. Our technology has so far outpaced our theology that we now face suicidal destruction if we use our weapons on others. Intercontinental missiles with nuclear warheads have made national states incapable of self-defense. Yet our Christian theology of war and peace has not even reached the age of the national state. We find ourselves almost silent members of a nation that threatens massive nuclear retaliation as its basic national policy.

It is out of this silence that William Durland speaks. He emphasizes the Christian witness to the gospel of peace by the mainstream of Christians during the first three centuries. The words of Athenagoras, Clement of Alexandria, Irenaeus, Origen, and others testify to this.

The change with Constantine's conversion and Augustine's just-unjust war theory is well documented. The continuing thread of theology of war is traced through St. Thomas and Pope Urban's Crusades up to and including Vatican II. The modern voices of Pope John, the Berrigan brothers, cardinals Alfrink and Ottaviani, Thomas Merton, and Martin Luther King are called as witnesses to testify to our need for a developed theology of peace.

The book was written originally as a long letter to the 1971 International Synod of Bishops meeting in Rome on the issues of peace and justice. It deserves the close attention of all who see Christ's teaching and example as important, all who want the human family to survive. If we become convinced of the truths expressed in this book, maybe we will follow the plea of Vatican II that we "strain every muscle as we work for the time when all war can be completely outlawed by international consent."

Richard T. McSorley, S.J.

Assistant Professor of Theology
and Roman Catholic Priest-Pacifist
Georgetown University
Washington, D.C.

Author's Preface

One of the major peace demonstrations protesting the Vietnam War took place in November 1969. It resulted in property damage, violence, and personal injury. I was practicing law in Washington, D.C., and concluding my second term in the Virginia state legislature at the time. For me it marked a change in my way of living.

I had grown up as a Roman Catholic and a patriotic American. My youthful heroes were the United States Marines and the Christian Knights of King Arthur's Round Table. In those years I would never have supported any demonstration designed to show that the United States was unjust in its international dealings. My formative years were influenced by World War II, a war in which this country sought to stamp out racial prejudice in Germany and to bring peace to the world. My scholastic natural law philosophy had convinced me of the higher morality of the right of the state to kill for peace. The philosophy of Aquinas had taught me that Catholics were obliged to participate in killing for the state, so I did not question the right of the United States to kill Vietnamese or injure anyone else as long as the war was just. I was convinced that the war was just because we were helping a smaller country that could not help itself. However, by the time of the 1969 demonstrations, I began to question whether the war in Vietnam was just. But the violence of the demonstrators did not seem just either. Maybe justice was not the answer.

Just before Christmas 1969, a little over a month after the peace demonstration, I came upon a little book called *The Wisdom of Tolstoy.*[1] I hesitated to buy it because its title reminded me of another famous book, *Wisdom of Mao.* I did not mind reading books justifying American violence, but I resented seeing books on the newsstands which justified communist violence. But the wisdom in the Tolstoy book was not violent. He wrote of love not of "justified violence." It was my first introduction to the Christian meaning of nonresistance of which Jesus spoke in Matthew 5:39.[2] I had never heard this particular verse on nonresistance interpreted in any church I attended. I recall a Catholic priest reading it in the 1950s as part of the gospel for that Sunday, but when it came time to give the sermon, the sermon was not on the Scripture but on a fund-raising letter from the bishop.

I undertook to study the Scriptures, particularly the Sermon on the Mount, and have been doing so ever since. I was changed politically and spiritually. I agreed with Leo Tolstoy that to "resist not the evildoer" meant just that. I no longer could understand why spiritual leaders such as Carl McIntire could come to Washington urging Americans to resist the evildoer, in what he called a just war and I could no longer understand how Thomas Aquinas and Augustine could disagree so violently with the clear meaning of these words of Jesus.

It was clear to me then that political demonstrations, even for peace, may erupt into violence, and that any demonstration designed to bring about only a change in politics generally fails. Politicians tend to be responsible only to their constituents. It dawned on me that we should not be demonstrating before politicians, but rather we should be directing our pleas to the consciences of the moral theologians, those who preach that it is just to kill in war.

I now believe that the teaching of Roman Catholicism is wrong on this fundamental precept of moral theology. Further study made me want to share my new Christian viewpoint with other Christians who for so long had been sheltered from the nonviolence of early Christianity. I realized I had been worshiping Caesar when I supported the just war. I should have been worshiping God and His Son Jesus, the Prince of Peace, instead.

I have written this book for committed Christians so that I might share my thoughts with them. The reader will find in these pages many arguments against the position I take. I quote fully Augustine and Aquinas and many others who disagree with what I have now found in my heart to be the true Christian philosophy concerning war and violence.

Those who become Christian pacifists are criticized by both left and right. Mao Tse-tung, Hitler, Stalin, Aquinas, Augustine, Niebuhr unanimously criticize pacifists for professing to know ahead of time that one can never participate in the use of violence. These advocates of "just" violence are upset because a Christian may say *a priori* that he is against violence whether it is just or unjust. They ask us to consider each situation on its merits looking at the justice of the event or the consequences of not using violence.

The Christian faith is not based only on the philosophical concept of justice or only on the philosophy of utilitarianism but rather on the virtue of love and the authority of Jesus. If we accept on faith what Jesus has asked of us, then the consequences are irrelevant. There can be no injustice flowing from following in His footsteps. Whatever the results, we know that they will be right as long as we do what Jesus says. This book suggests that for Christians to be Christians, we must return to the nonviolent witness of the New Testament.[3]

What would such a witness entail? There are some who say that, John, in writing Revelation had in mind Caesar when describing the anti-Christ as the beast. He said that the number of the beast was the number of a man, 666, or according to some authorities, 616. Greek and Hebrew letters have been equated with numbers, the value of the numbers corresponding to its numerical place in the alphabet. In order to determine the total number of a person's name, one would add the component letters, and by so doing, some biblical scholars have hypothesized that the Hebrew letters of Caesar-Nero add up to 666 and that the Greek letters for Caesar-God add up to 616.

It appears that John had a political power in mind for the Antichrist. Some writers today believe that John was writing for our own time and was not referring to a Caesar of the Romans but perhaps to a modern Caesar. In either case, the commentators warn us to be on our guard against those in political power who would ask us to disobey our Christian obligation to honor God over man. But for all of us, at some time, a conflict will arise concerning our duty to God and to men. Quite often the choice is more appropriately stated between God and Caesar. Caesar, as the ruler of men, asks for our allegiance and this request may conflict with our allegiance to God. This happened in the early centuries of Christianity when Christians were asked to honor Caesar in words by taking oaths of loyalty, and to honor him in action by taking up arms. Christians would do neither and gave up their lives instead.

They did neither because they believed the Sermon on the Mount required them to do no violence to any man, but rather to love all men, to pray for their enemies even if their enemy happened to be Caesar, to walk the extra mile, to give away their cloaks, but not to give Caesar their souls by disobeying the will of God. However, a time came when Christians were willing to reverse their early ways, swear allegiance to Constantine, and fight in his armies.

This book tells the story of what the author believes is the clear teaching of Jesus on the Sermon on the Mount, foretold by the prophets of the Old Testament and practiced by Him and by the saints of the early church.

Part one, "New Wineskins and Old: The Authority of Jesus," consists of three chapters. The first summarizes the book, while the second attempts to explain the teaching of the Sermon on the Mount in a novel and unusual way. This chapter, unlike other chapters which take a more analytical approach, attempts to take the reader back to the time of Jesus and the Sermon on the Mount so that he may feel the presence of the events in an existential way. The third chapter points to the Old Testament, particularly to Isaiah, as foretelling what actually took place in the early years of the first century. Part one, then, sets the biblical scene and emphasizes its pacifistic and nonresistant ethic.

Part two, "The Spirit and the Power: The Authority of Caesar," picks up the historical trends of the relationship between God, Caesar, and the Christian. Chapter four begins with the descent of the Holy Spirit upon the apostles and emphasizes their apostolic witness to the good news of peace. Chapter five gives attention to a part of Christian history most overlooked. The early Christians almost universally proclaimed a pacifistic witness. Today we hear so many diverse interpretations of biblical statements. Should we not consider how those first Christians understood the message of Christ? Such an examination leads us to the conclusion that if we truly intend to practice the teachings of Jesus, our lives must be devoted to peace both as a means as well as an end. But in chapter six we see a great reversal. Violence seeped into the church through the allegiance given to Constantine by the Christians in exchange for the toleration of their religion. From that beginning of Christian violence the book traces the history of anger, hate, war, and violence to our own day when Christians are not sure what Jesus asks of them.

Part three, "Quo Vadis: Jesus or Caesar?" is an analysis of the contemporary scene particularly of the violence and nonviolence of Roman Catholicism. Chapter seven examines a papal encyclical, the Vatican council and bishops' synod, and contemporary positions on the question of the just war and nonviolence. Chapter eight attempts to show the confusion of Christians, both Catholic and Protestant, regarding the nonviolent ethic with an emphasis again on Roman Catholicism. It questions whether contemporary Catholic peace movements are in accord with the pacifistic teachings of the early church. Chapter nine concludes the book with some vignettes and anecdotal references on the failure of violence and the "successful" practice of Christian love.

Christian nonviolence is much like the three great virtues of faith, hope, and love. To believe in nonviolence takes faith, to practice it demands love, and to follow through with it requires hope.

The purpose of this book is to help the reader see more clearly that Christians were not always violent, that Christ taught us to be nonviolent and loving simply because it is God's will, that Christians ought to assume the risk of nonviolence through faithfulness and hope for its eventual success either in this world or in the next. For Jesus taught us that whatever may be the eventual outcome of our faith and love, whether "success" or suffering, we should rejoice and be glad, for our reward will be great in heaven! From beginning to end this book simply calls Christians to reexamine the teachings of Jesus, and to ask once again how to practice faith, hope, and love according to our Father's will.

I would like to thank my mother, Lillian S. Durland, my wife, Lee, Pat Nicholson, Machaelle Wright, James and Betty Gilbert, Eugenia Halaby, Richard McSorley, Paul M. Schrock, J. Richard Burkholder, John A. Lapp, and Jan Hoagburg for their help in bringing this book to its final publication.

William R. Durland

Part I

New Wineskins and Old:
The Authority of Jesus

CHAPTER 1

No King but Caesar?

The Vietnam War has caused many Americans to question the justification of violence in Southeast Asia. Now that the war is over, at least for Americans, a larger question remains to be faced. Is any war justified? A great majority of those Americans who fought in the Vietnam War called themselves Christians. For centuries most Christians have conceded the morality of the just war without question, and when asked to fight "Caesar's" wars, they have unhesitatingly obeyed. But this has not always been the case. Prior to the toleration of Christianity by Constantine in AD 311, Christians were taught not to participate in wars and violence whether justified or not.

The early Christians accepted Jesus' teaching on love as precluding any violence whether it be abortion, infanticide, capital punishment, or war. They practiced the spirit of love for three centuries after which, with few exceptions, in the name of justice, they returned to the violence so typical of the time before Christ. What caused this radical reversion to violence? Why did it happen and why do we continue to mimic it?

This book tries to answer these questions and to ask Christians whether they know whom they are ultimately following, Christ or Caesar?

When Jesus was on trial, Pilate asked Him, "So you are a king then?" and Jesus said, "Yes, I am a king. I was born for this, I came into the world for this: to bear witness to the truth; and all who are on the side of truth listen to my voice." Later Pilate turned to the crowds and said, "Here is your king," but they answered, "Take Him away, take Him away! Crucify Him." But Pilate rejoined, "Do you want me to crucify your king?" The chief priests answered, "We have no king except Caesar." Jesus was then handed over to be crucified. (See John 18:37, 38 and 19:14-16.)

It is the thesis of this book that many present-day "chief priests" have no king but "Caesar." Why is this so today when the early Christians would rather have died than kill their enemy, whether he was Jew, pagan, or Roman? During the first 300 years after the time of Christ the Christian theologians of that day, Justin Martyr, Origen, Martin, Cyprian, and Clement taught that Christians should not kill either by abortion, by death penalty, or by war. But then Constantine-Caesar converted to Christianity, proclaimed Christianity as the religion of Rome, remained a warrior, and welcomed all Christians to participate in the government and the military. And from that time until the present, Christians have killed for "Rome" reinforced by the teachings of the Christian clergy. Now only a remnant of Christians refuse to kill for "Rome."

According to the gospel as related by Matthew, Jesus

testified in His Sermon on the Mount, "You must not kill; and if anyone does kill he must answer for it before the court. But I say this to you: anyone who is angry with his brother will answer for it before the court" (Mt. 5:21, 22). And further, "You have learned how it was said: Eye for eye and tooth for tooth. But I say this to you: offer the wicked man no resistance. On the contrary, if anyone hits you on the right cheek, offer him the other as well" (Mt. 5:38, 39). And again, "You have learned how it was said: You must love your neighbor and hate your enemy. But I say this to you: love your enemies and pray for those who persecute you" (Mt. 5:43, 44). For centuries, despite Christ's new and unique directive, men — including professed Christians — have promoted wars and violence as a just means for obtaining rights and redress. In the Roman Catholic Church, the years between Constantine and Pope John saw little change insofar as the promotion of the gospel of peace was concerned. The hierarchy became the standard-bearer for justified violence.

Finally, Vatican II announced far-reaching statements on war, and quietly questioned the just war theories of Augustine and Aquinas. In the process, however, Vatican II also stated that "as long as the danger of war remains and there is no competent and sufficiently powerful authority at the international level, governments cannot be denied the right to legitimate defense once every means of peaceful settlement has been exhausted"[1] and that "it is legitimate to refuse . . . to call for total renouncement of force by individual nations until an adequate security actually exists."[2]

The same document, however, does ask us to "undertake an evaluation of war with an entirely new attitude."[3] It reminds us that Pope John XXIII cautioned that "in an age such as ours which prides itself on its atomic energy, it is contrary to reason to believe that war is now a suitable way to restore rights which have been violated."[4]

The document concludes that divine providence urgently demands of us that we free ourselves from the age-old slavery of war.[5] "Those who are dedicated to the work of education, particularly of the young, or who mold public opinion, should regard as their most weighty task, the effort to instruct all in the fresh sentiments of peace."[6] No less does it speak out against individual and group violence where it states, "We cannot fail to praise those who renounce the use of violence in the vindication of their rights."[7] And again, "The teaching of Christ even requires that we forgive injuries, and extend the law of love to include every enemy according to the command of the new law.[8]

In September of 1971, the International Synod of Bishops, in union with the Catholic Commission on Peace and Justice, met in Rome to undertake further discussions on these weighty subjects. It was fervently hoped that these men who mold public opinion would regard as their grave task the effort to instruct all in the fresh sentiments of peace as enunciated by Vatican II. That Synod should have undertaken a complete restudy and reevaluation of the present Christian posture on war and peace to determine whether the church's present position is morally reconcilable with the teachings of Jesus Christ. If not, the International Synod of Bishops should have proclaimed to the world a statement of Christian conscience compatible with the peace gospel of the Sermon on the Mount. The Synod failed to act in that regard.

In the recent past, some lonely voices have urged the Catholic bishops to take such action. On the opening of the debate on peace and war at Vatican II, on November 10, 1964, Maximus IV, Patriarch of Antioch and Jerusalem, stated that "the intervention of 2,000 bishops from all parts of the world on behalf of peace could change the course of history and safeguard the fate of humanity. . . . We at the Council must make a declaration *urbi et orbi* (to the city and to the world), a declaration that will be plain, unambiguous, and precise."[9] The Council did not do this. A careful reading of the many writings which have analyzed the peace and war message of Vatican II indicates that such a statement has not been forthcoming and that it is long overdue.

Perhaps it is coincidence that it was Patriarch Maximus who urged the world in the twentieth century to a lifestyle commensurate with that lived by Maximilian of the third century. Maximilian, a young African, was summoned before a proconsul of Rome to serve in the army. Apparently as the son of an army veteran he was one of the few persons in the realm who had an obligation to serve. He refused to accept the soldier's badge on the grounds that he was a Christian, and for that reason could not serve as a soldier and do evil. He was told that there were other Christians in the army. He replied, "They know what is fitting for them: but I am a Christian, and I cannot do evil." As he was led away to his execution, he said, "My arms are with the Lord. I cannot fight for any earthly consideration. I am now a Christian.[10] Maximilian died in AD 295, a martyr. He was buried close to the grave of St. Cyprian, an earlier patristic father and church pacifist, who died in AD 258 proclaiming that "if a murder is committed privately, it is a crime, but if it happens with state authority, courage is the name for it."[11]

From Maximilian to Maximus a remnant of Christians have cried out for peace. But we have proclaimed peace only as an end and not as a means. And this is the key. All committed Christians must recognize peace as the means as well as the end. There is no way to peace; peace is the way.

Protestant and Orthodox traditions have offered little more than Roman Catholics in the practice of Christian nonviolence. With the exception of small Christian communities such as the Mennonites, the Brethren, and the Quakers (known as the historic peace churches), the major Protestant and Orthodox branches of Christendom from the Reformation on accepted without question the theory of justified violence.

We must also remember in analyzing the historic growth of the cancer of violence that the pre-Reformation church was the Roman Catholic Church. So the greatest responsibility for sowing violent seeds prior to the Reformation must rest with that church. By the time of the Reformation, the issue of violence and nonviolence was not a decisive factor in the Protestant revolt. Luther, Calvin, and the pope all accepted violence as a justified means to a good end. The issue was not whether to kill but whom to kill.

After the Reformation the Protestants became so diffused that no one organization can speak for them all. Those denominations emerging from the Calvinist and Lutheran traditions accepted violence. Those denominations emerging from the Anabaptist branch generally rejected it. For these reasons greater emphasis has been placed in our discussion on the theory and practice of Roman Catholicism in relation to violence and nonviolence than on the Protestant tradition.

If we are to follow in the nonviolent footsteps of Jesus, there can be no participation in war and violence for Christians, just as there was none for the early Christians.

In our age many Christians have lost sight of their nonviolent King and have no king but violent "Caesar." In recent years Christians have been asked whether God is dead.

Perhaps the more important question is whether Christians are dead. Would a return to the spirit of early Christianity bring life to Christians again? No better start could be made than to restudy the words of Jesus.

CHAPTER 2

The King of the Christians

The Suffering Servant

Let us for a moment drift back 2,000 years to a sloping hill in Palestine on a warm, breezy day when Jesus sat down to talk to His new followers about a lifestyle for the future. This lifestyle would not resemble that of the religious leaders of His time who preached that the anger of God was acted out in the anger of men. Perhaps gathered around this small group were bystanders who felt it a little too hot to work that day but cool enough to listen.

Jesus spoke in the context of three political organizations: the politics of Rome, the government of Herod, and the theocracy of the Jewish religionists. The first was based on the sword of Rome, the second on the political conniving of Herod to retain his power at any cost, and the third on the fire and brimstone of the Old Testament. The people of Palestine had listened to various prophets crying out in the wilderness against Rome. But here was one who was different, one who would become a suffering servant as foretold by Isaiah, and not a political power symbol.

Time moved more slowly in that age so a person could spend a few hours on a hillside listening to one more Jewish prophet, particularly if he had any new ideas about overcoming the foreign, political regimes of Rome or the local political regime of Herod. Certainly the Old Testament spoke of violent force even though the Lord told the Jews, "Vengeance is mine." Perhaps a leader would come along finally who would be a Messiah modeled after David the king or Solomon the judge. Kings and judges are the men who change the world, are they not, from one political regime to another? Some Jews were anxious for a new political order. After all, hadn't God sided with the Israelites against the Egyptians? Hadn't God smote the Egyptian people, and killed Egyptian babies? Hadn't their God delivered them into the promised land and enabled them to wrest it from the hands of the Canaanites? Would Jesus tell them about such a God who would lead them against a political foe? Would Jesus tell them that He, as a political Messiah, would take over the throne of the land and drive out the enemy?

His followers knew that He had been tempted by the devil in the wilderness — tempted with the lure of physical security, material possessions, popular favor, and political power. But He turned His back on material riches, popular esteem, and worldly power. What message would be forthcoming now that could change the world without recourse to possessions, property, popularity, or power?

His followers look interested. Let's listen too. What is He saying?

"How happy are the poor in spirit;
their's is the kingdom of heaven.
Happy the gentle:
they shall have the earth for their heritage.
Happy those who mourn:
they shall be comforted.
Happy those who hunger and thirst for what is right:
they shall be satisfied.
Happy the merciful:
they shall have mercy shown them.
Happy the pure in heart:
they shall see God.
Happy the peacemakers:
they shall be called sons of God.
Happy those who are persecuted in the cause of right:
theirs is the kingdom of heaven.
"Happy are you when people abuse you and persecute you and speak all kinds of calumny against you on my account. Rejoice and be glad for your reward will be great in heaven; this is how they persecuted the prophets before you" (Mt. 5:3-12).

What! No mention of power — political or otherwise? No mention of property or possessions? Don't try to be popular, He says. He tells us how to be happy, but it seems difficult. The Old Testament negatives are heavy enough, but now He makes the rules even heavier. The Old says you must not kill and that if anyone does kill he must answer for it before the court. But now Jesus says: "Anyone who is angry with his brother will answer for it before the court" (Mt. 5:22). Someone in the crowd protests, "That can't be. A little anger is good." Another observes, "Righteous anger is good, but who knows when anger is righteous? Is He saying not to be angry because we don't know when it's justified?" No, He couldn't be saying that. He advocates forsaking anger for something more powerful. Perhaps He's going to organize an army.

Jesus proceeds. He refers again to Moses and the Jewish ancestors. "You have learned how it was said: Eye for eye and tooth for tooth. But I say this to you: offer the wicked man no resistance. On the contrary, if anyone hits you on the right cheek, offer him the other as well: if a man takes you to law and would have your tunic, let him have your cloak as well. And if anyone orders you to go one mile, go two miles with him. Give to anyone who asks, and if anyone wants to borrow, do not turn away" (Mt. 5:38-42).

"This can't be," one bystander protests. "We didn't hear Him right. We've always been taught that it's just to exact an eye for an eye and a tooth for a tooth. If we allow someone to hit us on the right cheek and do not resist, we are perpetuating his evil in not resisting it. And as far as borrowers are concerned, if we give them money without determining whether it will be used properly, we'll be contributing to future evil. And besides, don't we have a right to make sure we'll be paid back? What kind of a message is this?"

Jesus continues. "You have learned how it was said: You must love your neighbor and hate your enemy. But I say this to you: love your enemies and pray for those who persecute you: in this way you will be sons of your Father in heaven, for he causes his sun to rise on bad men as well as good, and his rain to fall on honest and dishonest men alike. For if you love those who love you, what right have you to claim any credit? Even the tax collectors do as much, do they not? And if you save your greetings for your brothers, are you doing anything exceptional? Even the pagans do as much, do they not? You must therefore be perfect just as your heavenly Father is perfect" (Mt. 5:43-48).

"What does He mean, perfect? I can see this ethic

as an ideal. I can see it as a temporary lifestyle. But to be perfect this cannot be. And who is He to ask it of us? Apparently He doesn't even know our heavenly Father because our heavenly Father told us to hate our enemies. If you love your enemy, you have no one to hate! He's telling us not to rise up against the Romans. If we love our enemies we'll be called sons of God. And He says we should treat others as we would like them to treat us. This is the meaning of the law and the prophets. Would we like someone to kill us? If not, don't kill anyone. Would we like someone to break into our house and destroy our property? If not, don't break into their house or destroy their property. This isn't practical. I believe righteous anger sometimes demands it. Righteousness even allows killing the evil doer. But this Man has said not to do any of these things!"

Jesus finished speaking and His teaching made a deep impression on those people because He taught them with authority. The crowd dispersed, some of them saying, "From whom does He get His authority? We must watch this man. Remember, he admonished us that everyone who listens to His words and acts upon them will be like a sensible man who built his house on rock. But everyone who listens to His words and does not act upon them will be like a stupid man who built his house on sand. (See Matthew 7:24-27.) Let's watch Him awhile before we act on His words. Perhaps He's a Zealot in disguise. He'll probably turn violent. Maybe He's just hiding under this peaceful cover. Maybe He will lead us to a revolution. Let's stick close to Him because He may be the key to overthrowing Rome and freeing our conquered people."

So Jesus was followed by some who were curious whether He would lead them in revolt. They continued to muse. "There's a good case for revolution. We're an angry people and not without reason. Perhaps He will unite us and overthrow this political government. That certainly would be the justice He spoke about on the hill. But He hasn't made a move in that direction. Why doesn't He set us free from slavery to Rome? Why doesn't He overthrow the government? Isn't that what a Messiah should do?"

A year or so passes, and the same followers are asking themselves more questions. They are puzzled over Jesus saying, "When the Son of Man comes in his glory . . . all the nations will be assembled. . . . He will place the sheep on his right hand and the goats on his left. Then the King witl say . . . 'Come, you whom my Father has blessed, take for your heritage the kingdom prepared for you since the foundation of the world. For I was hungry and you gave me food; I was thirsty and you gave me drink; I was a stranger and you made me welcome; naked and you clothed me, sick and you visited me, in prison and you came to see me.' Then the virtuous will say to him in reply, 'Lord, when did we see you . . . a stranger and make you welcome; naked and clothe you; sick or in prison and go to see you?' and the King will answer: 'I tell you solemnly, in so far as you did this to one of the least of these brothers of mine, you did it to me.' Next he will say to those on his left hand, 'Go away from me. . . . For I was hungry and you never gave me food; I was thirsty and you never gave me anything to drink; I was a stranger and you never made me welcome, naked and you never clothed me, sick and in prison and you never visited me.' Then it will be their turn to ask, 'Lord, when did we see you hungry or thirsty, a stranger or naked, sick or in prison, and did not come to your help?' Then he will answer, 'I tell you solemnly, in so far as you neglected to do this to one of the least of these, you neglected to do it to me' " (Mt. 25:31-45).

But this is folly. Feeding the hungry, going to prisons. He's not a violent revolutionary. How can He expect to gain any followers? And what a believer in law and order. Just the other day, He caused a fuss at the Temple, driving out all those who were selling and buying there, upsetting the tables of the money changers and the chairs of those who were peddling pigeons. And He recited Scripture to them: "My house will be called a house of prayer; but you are turning it into a robbers' den" (Mt. 21:13).

"Now there's violence," someone observed. "Finally He's coming out."

"The sellers had no right to be there," another protested. "He overturned their tables as He drove out the cattle but He didn't harm man or beast. He enforced the law. He did not disobey it."

"Well, I don't know, we'll have to talk more on this. It doesn't seem to coincide with His previous lifestyle. My guess is violence will come soon. Rome beware!"

Not long after, one of those who had been following Jesus and observing His lifestyle reported that He had instructed His apostles to buy two swords. (See Luke 22:35-38.) Now they were sure He would use violence. The authorities were coming to apprehend him. "We must be there at the time of the arrest. Because He is so peaceful, they do not know His followers possess swords. You can be sure He will use them when they attempt to arrest Him, and then the revolution surely will begin." So they watched to see what would happen. Judas, accompanied by a large number of men armed with swords and clubs, pointed Jesus out to the priests and elders. The men seized Jesus and led Him away. But at that point "one of the followers of Jesus grasped his sword and drew it; he struck out at the high priest's servant, and cut off his ear. Jesus then said, 'Put your sword back, for all who draw the sword will die by the sword' " (Mt. 26:51, 52). And then He healed the fellow's ear.

"There He goes again," an observer may have said, "telling someone to get a sword and then commanding him not to use it. What is this all about?"

We know the story well. Jesus did not resist arrest. He was convicted and crucified. He returned and instructed His apostles, "Go, therefore, and make disciples of all the nations; baptize them in the name of the Father and of the Son and of the Holy Spirit, and teach them to observe all the commands I gave you" (Mt. 28:19, 201.

And this is what priests and ministers must do to this day if they would follow Him. They must teach the commands to love one's enemies, to resist not the evildoer, to refrain from anger of any kind, whether "Caesar" likes it or not. All the writings and teachings of Jesus can be summed up simply by the words, "Love God and love one another." Surely we know that it is impossible to love another if we set out to kill him. Like the Jews surrounding Pilate, we always seem to choose Barabbas (a Zealot who advocated secret murder and violent overthrow of the foreign government) instead of Jesus. But Christ's message was so powerful that He could unite as apostles of peace both Matthew, who ardently cooperated with the Roman system, and Simon, the Zealot, who had worked just as hard to overthrow the Roman Order.

The peace of Jesus is not what we at first might think. It is not yet the peace of nations, but the peace of persons. It is in this world but not of this world. It may prove successful or unsuccessful as far as the world is concerned, but we are to practice it nevertheless. It begins by loving God and one another. Nations simply cannot love nations until we love one another. When that love grows, it can envelop nations and the world because its power is supernatural. But it must be practiced by applying the Sermon on the Mount in our lives. Can those who urge us not to practice it, convince us that Jesus was not a pacifist?

Violence and the Temple

Two major propositions are put forth to demonstrate that Jesus was not a pacifist. One focuses on His supposedly violent acts at the Temple. The other maintains that the Sermon on the Mount, although obviously nonviolent and pacifistic, was not intended to be acted out as a lifestyle, that it is not binding on any individual Christian. We shall examine both these arguments although not in detail because they have been dealt with frequently by numerous experts before some of whom are mentioned below. The cleansing of the Temple, especially as recorded in John, causes some people to conclude that Jesus was a Man capable of righteous anger and of aggressive personal violence, and that His actions at the Temple justify war and violence.

Cecil John Cadoux, in his treatise, *The Early Church and the World*, analyzes nonviolence and Jesus in the Temple in the following perspective:

> Christ so understood His own special mission as to refrain from all acts of hostility or severity towards human beings. The expulsion of the traders from the Temple courts, which is often regarded as the one significant exception to this general statement, proves on careful examination not to be so. The whip appears only in the fourth Gospel, and even there, an actual exegesis represents it as used upon the cattle and not upon the men. The treatment of the latter is described in four Gospels by a Greek word which means no more than authoritative dismissal or dispatch as is clear from other uses made of it. It is impossible in the nature of things for one man to drive out a crowd by physical force or even by the threat of it. What he can do is to overawe them by his presence and personality and expel them by an authoritative command, and that apparently was what Jesus did. The idea that with the help of His disciples He over-

> powered the traders, in a sort of pitched battle, has no foundation whatever in the Gospel narrative.[1]

Furthermore, if Jesus posed a violent threat, why wasn't He immediately arrested by the Temple guards? Instead, after He had shamed the traders into leaving, blind and lame people came to the Temple where He cured them. "At the sight of the wonderful things he did and of the children shouting, 'Hosanna to the Son of David' in the Temple, the chief priests and the scribes were indignant. 'Do you hear what they are saying?' they said to him. 'Yes,' Jesus answered, 'have you never read this: By the mouths of children, babes in arms, you have made sure of praise?' " (Mt. 21:15, 15). All this took place on the same day. Lame people, blind people, children, and Pharisees gathered around this "violent" Man. With that, He left them and went out of the city to Bethany where He spent that night. He returned to the city in the early morning. And by this time the Pharisees had some questions for Him. "He had gone into the Temple and was teaching, when the chief priests and the elders of the people came to him and said, 'What authority have you for acting like this? And who gave you this authority?' (Mt. 20:23). Whereupon a clever discourse between the Pharisees and Jesus ensued.

It is apparent that Jesus was neither violent nor warlike. He calls Himself "meek and humble" and we should believe Him. It is further apparent that whatever He was doing, He was doing under the auspices of His divine authority. Christ advises us to love our enemies and not to resist the evildoer. We are told in the Old Testament that vengeance belongs to God not man (Lev. 19:18 and Deut. 32:35). Paul also emphasizes this in Romans 12:19. It should be clear, except for those who wish to rationalize the justification of violence of property and of persons, that Jesus in the Temple was demonstrating that His religious authority over the Temple and the Pharisees is based on His divine nature, something which none of us possesses.

The Meaning of the Sermon on the Mount

Thus we are left with the pacifism of the Sermon on the Mount. Several arguments have been formulated which hold that we should not apply it literally to our lives. The first of these is that the Sermon is an attempt to replace the Old Testament legalism with a New Testament spirit, that to draw a literal interpretation from the New Testament at any point, including the Sermon on the Mount, would create a new legalism. This argument is very interesting. One wonders why the churches which have established literal doctrines based on other quotations from the New Testament do not apply such literalism consistently throughout the New Testament. In any case, Jesus said that all the commandments could be summarized in one: Love God and love your neighbor. He admonished us that he whoever says he loves God and does not love his neighbor, is a liar. In fact, as we see from His comparisons between anger and killing, resistance and nonresistance, hating the enemy and loving the enemy. He imposes even stricter commands than those found in the Old Testament. But these are commands of discipleship, not law.

As Hans Windisch says in *The Meaning of the Sermon on the Mount:*

> The religion of the Sermon on the Mount, like that of Judaism, is predominantly a religion of "works" and of eschatological salvation. . . . The commands of the Sermon on the Mount are conditions of admittance addressed to men who wish to serve God and who yearn for the Kingdom. . . . It teaches an ethic that requires obedience and the fulfillment of specific demands. . . . It is obvious that the commands were intended to be obeyed. . . . It is Christ's ethic of obedi-

ence and of judgment. This is the theological character of the Sermon with which theological exegesis has to reckon. At this point it must make an important decision. Is it to regard the Sermon on the Mount as a binding authority, or is it to be free to employ the Sermon as it wishes? In the former instance it must regard the Law, the doctrine of obedience, the assumption that the commands are capable of fulfillment, and the postulate that obedience is the condition of salvation as authoritative elements of the universal Christian gospel. If it holds another idea of the Law, of the gospel, and of salvation, it must admit just as unreservedly that it no longer considers the ethic and the doctrine of salvation of the Sermon on the Mount in their original form as normative. Since Jesus completed his work in Jerusalem, since the Passion, since Easter and Pentecost, we can accept only certain parts of the Sermon as the divine proclamation. . . . Another foundation for its commands and promises has to be laid. From time to time there have been Christians who have chosen the former alternative. Tolstoy is by no means their only representative. Many Baptists belong to this group, and they cannot simply be dismissed as "fanatics" and "sectarians." If this is what they are, then Jesus himself was a fanatic and the founder of a sect. The unmistakable conclusion of our exegesis is that such people have correctly understood the Sermon on the Mount. The Sermon intends to proclaim commands. It presents demands that are to be literally understood and literally fulfilled. Polemic against "fanatics" is to a large extent polemic against the Sermon on the Mount and criticism of Jesus himself.[2]

Cadoux informs us:

But even the Pauline Epistles, not to mention the Synoptic Gospels, teach us that there is such a thing as "the Law of Christ, which while springing from "the Spirit of life in Christ Jesus" issues in certain very definite and concrete principles of conduct. . . . Who, for instance, would even allude that our Lord's prohibitions of adultery and unchastity could or ought to be disobeyed in the letter, while being observed in the spirit?[3]

Certainly it is true that the New Testament is a Scripture of the spirit, and the Old Testament is a Scripture of the Law. How then can we say that the Sermon on the Mount is a commandment to be obeyed much in the same way as Deuteronomy and Exodus and Leviticus set down specific commandments to be obeyed? The Old Testament laid down specific commands which, if broken, were immediately punishable by the theocracy of the times which had the power of civil authority. If a man injured another man's eye, he himself could be punished in like manner by the theocratic authorities. The spirit of the New Testament is one of freedom from the Law. We are admonished not to judge or condemn our neighbor. Although Jesus came not to abolish the law of the prophets, He did come to complete it. The man who infringes even one of the least of the commandments mentioned in the Sermon on the Mount, will be considered least in the kingdom of heaven. The man who keeps and teaches them will be considered great in the kingdom of heaven. He says to love our enemies and pray for those who persecute us and in this way we will be sons of our Father in heaven. He does not say that if our enemy harms us, some theocracy here on earth will punish him as was the case under the old dispensation. Most likely some autocracy or democracy will punish one if his sin (such as stealing) has a corresponding penalty in civil law. But that is a secular punishment. Since the Sermon on the Mount Christians should no longer consider the use of religious punishments as ethically valid under the guise of some Scripture.

We know that some Christians, in spite of the spirit of the Sermon on the Mount, continued to punish people for religious sins through inquisitions, crusades, and capital punishment, even utilizing the facilities of civil authority. Aquinas said that if the civil authority could take a man's life for stealing, no less should the religious authority be able to take a man's life as a heretic. In doing so, the man's life will be lost, but his soul will be saved.

But what is the spirit of Jesus? Jesus sets down a norm for us to accept, although we have free choice, and we alone determine our course. No longer has any religious or temporal authority on earth the right to exact an eye for an eye for a "religious" sin. So the law and the prophets have been fulfilled as far as the condemnation of the Old Testament law is concerned. Jesus says not to condemn anyone anymore. He continues to condemn the evil but not the evildoer, to condemn sin but not the sinner. Thus His example should lead us to "offer the wicked man no resistance." He never punished an evildoer. He never criticized a single Pharisee by name. But this does not mean that Jesus does not require us to follow our conscience. For not to speak out against evil would also be a sin under the New Testament. So Jesus speaks out against promiscuity, but He does not punish the promiscuous. He speaks out against the Pharisees, but He does not condemn any one Pharisee. The new commandment of love does not require it. The new commandment of love, however, does require us to follow the Sermon on the Mount and to teach all nations to do the same, but never does it require us to force nations or persons to do the same by means of punishment or retaliation.

Others say that the Sermon on the Mount is simply an ideal which none of us can attain, that it is impossible for us to be perfect, that Jesus never intended that any of us should strive to make those commandments part of our lifestyle. Yet He told us that not all those who say Lord, Lord — not all those who have performed miracles, cast out devils, or prophesied — will enter the kingdom of heaven, but those who listen to His words and *act* upon them. (See Matthew 7:21-23.) He says this near the end of the Sermon on the Mount and also admonishes, "You must therefore be perfect just as your heavenly Father is perfect" (Mt. 5:48). If Jesus said we must act on these words and asks us to be perfect, His standard must be attainable. If it is attainable for one, it may be attainable for all with the help of God the Father, Jesus Christ, and the Holy Spirit.

Lloyd-Jones in his *Studies in the Sermon on the Mount* maintains that if the Sermon is to apply at all, it is for the individual and not intended for communities or nations.[4] By this interpretation, Christ's Sermon is applicable to an individual who may wish to follow the Sermon on the Mount in his own life but is not binding when he becomes a soldier under the authority of the state. Unfortunately, this view holds the authority of the state to be superior to the authority of the Sermon on the Mount, and places the law of men above the law of God against the clear statement to the contrary by Peter and the apostles in Acts. Granted the Sermon on the Mount cannot be legislated at the United Nations by majority vote, and thereafter made binding on the minority. But the Sermon on the Mount is binding on all Christians as individuals who are part of communities of nations.

Some theologians argue that Romans 13 where Paul asks us to obey the government sets the rule for the role of the Christian in public ethics and Matthew 5 for personal ethics. John H. Yoder in his recent book, *The Politics of Jesus,* corrects this error. Analyzing Romans he states:

> Verse 7 says, "Render to each his *due*"; verse 8 says, "Nothing is *due* to anyone except love." Thus the claims of Caesar are to be measured by whether what he claims is due to him is part of the obligation of love. Love in turn is defined (v. 10) by the fact that it does no harm. In this context it therefore becomes impossible to maintain that the subjection referred to in verses 1-7 can include a moral

> obligation under certain circumstances to do harm to others at the behest of government. . . . Romans 12—13 and Matthew 5—7 are not in contradiction or in tension. They *both* instruct Christians to be nonresistant in all their relationships, including the social. They *both* call on the disciples of Jesus to renounce participation in the interplay of egoisms which this world calls "vengeance" or "justice." They *both* call Christians to respect and be subject to the historical process in which the sword continues to be wielded and to bring about a kind of order under fire, but not to perceive in the wielding of the sword their own reconciling ministry.[5]

There is nothing in the New Testament or the Sermon on the Mount which indicates that the commandments proclaimed by Jesus are subject to qualification by the state.

Another argument is that the teachings of the Sermon on the Mount on nonresistance were binding only until the *parousia*, that is, until the expected return of Jesus within a few years after His resurrection. Indeed, many believed that Jesus would return shortly, but the writings of the apostles and patristic fathers did not teach that the Christian should be nonresistant only because Christians would not have to be that way very long. None of the early church fathers indicated that their abhorrence for violence in war and their adherence to pacifism was based on the expectation of an early reward. Indeed, Lactantius around AD 300, much later than the expected *parousia*, said, "Man is so sacrosanct a creature that it is always wrong to kill him. . . . No exception can be made to this commandment of God."[6] Lactantius recognized that this teaching was more than an ideal. It was not only spirit but commandment as well, binding on all — soldier and civilian, slave and free man.

Three final arguments, although minor, should be mentioned. Augustine wrote that the Sermon is only binding on the soul and not on outward acts. This argument seems to abolish the teaching altogether, for however holy a thought may be, it is holier still when acted upon. Others flatly say, "The question of killing and taking of life is not considered as such in this teaching."[7] This statement is naive indeed, for throughout the Sermon anger, hatred, killing, resistance, persecution, and peacemaking are discussed explicitly. A final contemporary argument holds that "we cannot solve ethical questions of the twentieth century by looking at what Jesus did in the first. . . . The Christian does not decide between violence and nonviolence, evil and good. He decides between less and greater evil. He must ponder whether revolutionary violence is less or more deplorable than the violence perpetuated by the system. There are no absolute rules which can decide the answer with certainty."[8] These last three arguments seem to be grasping at straws to find any reason not to apply the very radical lifestyle Jesus requests.

Is the Sermon on the Mount valid in the twentieth century? The Sermon on the Mount has been recognized by psychiatrists as a valid and practical guideline for real life. Dr. James T. Fisher tells us:

> Not until I took up the study of psychiatry did I pause to consider deeply the significance of religious ritual and to ponder its value to the world. . . . I examined many patients who could recite long passages from the Bible, but none who could honestly understand the basic philosophy of what he was reciting, and none who had lived in accordance with the rules being quoted. . . . I could never be entirely satisfied with my role as a psychiatrist, struggling to find a sage pathway so that I might lead a few lost souls out of the wilderness of mental abnormality. What was needed, I felt sure, was some new and enlightened recipe for living a sane and satisfying life. . . .
>
> I dreamed of writing a handbook that would be simple, practical, easy to understand, easy to follow. It would tell

people how to live — what thoughts and attitudes and philosophies to cultivate, and what pitfalls to avoid in seeking mental health. I attended every symposium that was possible for me to attend and took notes on the wise words of my teachers and of my colleagues who were leaders in their field. And quite by accident I discovered that such a work had already been completed!

If you were to take the sum total of all authoritative articles ever written by the most qualified of psychologists and psychiatrists on the subject of mental hygiene — if you were to combine them and refine them and cleave out the excess verbiage — if you were to take the whole of the meat and none of the parsley, and if you were to have these unadulterated bits of pure scientific knowledge concisely expressed by the most capable of living poets, you would have an awkward and incomplete summation of the Sermon on the Mount. And it would suffer immeasurably through comparison.

For nearly two thousand years the Christian world has been holding in its hands the complete answer to its restless and fruitless yearnings. Here . . . rests the blueprint for successful human life with optimum mental health and contentment.[9]

Raymond L. Cramer mentions some interesting things which are relevant to our discussion of the teachings of the Sermon on the Mount. Jesus tells us to beware of anger not only righteous anger but anger itself. Cramer tells us that:

Anger is discussed in detail in the writings of Jesus, even as in psychiatric literature. Anger is one of the major causes of loss of equilibrium within the personality. It is a destructive force. There is always the danger of anger being present, especially if there is not a healthy supply of love and affection. These feelings bring about a physical breakdown as well as emotional conflict and interfere with interpersonal relationships. Some psychologists find this trait to be one of the most damaging in marriage. So it is no wonder that the psychology of Jesus and His concept of anger identifies with the flavor of present-day literature on the subject of anger.[10]

Cramer goes on to tell us:

> There is a special mechanism called the blood-brain barrier which screens out substances harmful to the brain. The tragedy is that certain gases, some medications, and especially alcohol pass through the barrier and many of these can do irreparable damage to the delicate brain cells. However, it would be safe to say, I believe, that *the most damaging factors not controlled by the blood-brain barrier are the thoughts that represent various sick emotional reactions* — these find ready access to the stimulation of the electrical impulses of the brain cells. How true is the teaching of the Bible that as a man thinketh in his heart, or mind, so is he! His thoughts can control his entire body — because the brain cells are subjected to the stimulation of thought patterns.[11]

Cramer concludes that the psychology of Jesus gives us a lifestyle based on love. And the psychiatrist tells us that love is at the crux of the conception of personality.[12] It would therefore seem that the theologian who wishes to relegate the Sermon on the Mount to an ideal or to an ethic which is outdated in the twentieth century, must contend with these psychiatrists and psychologists who tell us it is the only true way to live and order our daily lives.

That day under those trees, on the hill where the Sermon on the Mount was revealed, Jesus told us always to treat others as we would like them to treat us. This is the meaning of the law and the prophets. But suppose we do not care to treat others as we would want them to treat us, and do not look for kindness in return. The Golden Rule really does not require those who wish nothing in return to give anything at all. After Jesus had demonstrated the Sermon on the Mount by His own life, He left with us a commandment which gives us an even higher standard to follow. He said, "A new commandment I give to you, that you love one another; even as I have loved you, that you also love one another. By this all men will know that you are my disciples, if you have love for one another" (Jn. 13:34, 35, RSV). Jesus did not tell us to love others as we would have them love us. He told us to love others *as He had loved us,* that by so doing, all men would know His disciples.

Where are these Christians who have so loved one another that they can be identified as disciples of Jesus? Loving one another does not mean to love only your family, only your community, only your nation — which is hard enough — but to love your enemies whomever they may be, whether they are Americans, Chinese, or Russians, Jews, Negroes, or Indians, powerful, militant, peaceful, or weak — we must love them all. We must not subject them to violence. This is the teaching of the New Testament gospel of peace.

Centuries earlier, the Old Testament foretold and demonstrated the futility of violence, as we shall see in the next chapter.

CHAPTER 3

A Mark on Cain: Nonviolence in the Old Testament

Not so long ago on television, a couple whose child had been murdered were interviewed by a news reporter. The reporter wanted to know the reaction of the parents toward the murderer. The parents said they were Christians, and believed in the teachings of Jesus Christ. They felt that the murderer should give his life for that of their child because Jesus taught that one may require an eye for an eye and a tooth for a tooth.

Although in error about Christ's teaching, the parents were sincere and felt in their grief they were applying Christian teaching to the great moral tragedy which befell them. This example illustrates the lack of understanding many people have about the meaning of Christ's teaching. Matthew clearly states that the Old Testament command of an eye for an eye and a tooth for a tooth was radically changed by Jesus in the Sermon on the Mount. Rather we are to offer the wicked man no resistance and even to turn the other cheek (see Matthew 5:38, 39). Why do persons appeal to Old Testament quotations to prove that Christians are justified in practicing war and violence? Perhaps it is because we have heard so often that Yahweh, the Jewish God of war, gave a homeland to the promised people through bloodshed and strife. How can the Old Testament God be a God of war and the New Testament God a God of peace?

The early Christians looked upon the basic teachings of the Old Testament as fulfilled in the teachings of Jesus. The Old Testament was indeed an improvement on prior ethical concepts.

Early people lived by the law of the jungle, motivated by self-preservation. But eventually man found that it was not best in his own self-interest to seek his own self-interest at all times. If he killed ruthlessly, he would be killed ruthlessly. So some order was necessary. The Code of Hammurabi in 2100 BC was perhaps man's first systemized attempt to order this relationship with his fellowman. A man might be put to death, but only for certain reasons prescribed in the code. For example, if a man accused another of manslaughter and then could not prove it against him, the accuser was put to death. If a man kidnapped the infant son of a free man, he was put to death. If a man broke into a house and committed robbery, he was put to death. [1]

The law on killing in Deuteronomy and Leviticus in the Old Testament was similar to the Code of Hammurabi. A man's life could not be taken indiscriminately. The penalty should somehow fit the crime — an eye for an eye and a tooth for a tooth. Jesus fulfilled this law through His death. He taught that we should no longer live under that law but under grace. Henceforth, the law of justice would be replaced by the law of love.

Are we able to find this stream of love, fulfilled in the teachings of the Sermon on the Mount, in the history of the Old Testament? I believe we can.

Adam and Eve conceived and gave birth to Cain. And later a second child, Abel, was born. Cain became the first murderer by killing his brother. What was his earthly punishment? Neither Adam nor Yahweh killed Cain. Instead Yahweh banished Cain and made him a fugitive and wanderer over the earth. Cain said to the Lord "Whoever comes across me will kill me!" and Yahweh replied, "'If anyone kills Cain, sevenfold vengeance shall be taken for him.' So Yahweh put a mark on Cain to prevent whoever might come across him from striking him down" (Gen. 4:15, 16). What was the mark? It was something which prevented others from doing violence to Cain. Was he henceforth meek, nonresistant, forgiving? Whatever the case, we know that nowhere is it recorded that Cain was killed or that he ever killed again. His life was spared and the God of nonviolence protected a murderer from the justice of an eye for an eye.

Let us take a huge leap to the time of Moses, the greatest of Jewish leaders. In the Book of Acts Stephen tells us of Moses and his adopted life in Egypt, and of his eventual yearning to return to his brethren.

> At the age of forty he decided to visit his countrymen, the sons of Israel. When he saw one of them being ill-treated he went to his defense and rescued the man by killing the Egyptian. He thought his brothers realized that through him God would liberate them, but they did not. The next day, when he came across some of them fighting, he tried to reconcile them. "Friends," he said, "you are brothers; why are you hurting each other?" But the man who was attacking his fellow countryman pushed him aside. "And who appointed you," he said, "to be our leader and judge? Do you intend to kill me as you killed the Egyptian yester-

> day?" Moses fled when he heard this and he went to stay in the land of Midian, where he became the father of two sons. Acts 7:23-29.

A man will not be recognized as a peacemaker if he does violence, even if that violence is directed toward a good end. Moses practiced violence instead of nonviolence and was rejected. When Stephen told the story to the Jews who were interrogating him, and later killed him, they accused him of blaspheming Moses and God. They did not understand that the Old Testament from Cain to Moses to Isaiah anticipated the suffering servant of nonviolence, Jesus Christ.

Near the end of his life Jacob commented on the violence of his sons, Simeon and Levi. He said, "Let my soul not enter into their counsel nor my heart join in their company, for in their rage they have killed men" (Gen. 49:6).

Later David the king, a mighty warrior, assembled all the leaders of Israel at Jerusalem. These included the officials of the tribes, the officers of the divisions that served the king, the stewards of all the property and cattle of the king, his sons, together with the palace officials, and all the seasoned warriors. David told them he wanted to build a house for the Ark of the Covenant of the Lord, a place to worship God, and that he had planned such a building. "I have made preparations for building, but God has said to me, 'You are not to build a house for my name, for you have been a man of war and have shed blood' " (1 Chron. 28:3). So it was that not David, the warrior, but Solomon, the judge, was instructed by God to build a house of God. And God made Solomon king because he had not asked for longlife, possessions, wealth, honor, or the life of those who hated him, but had asked for wisdom and knowledge for himself that he might rule God's people over whom God had made him king. (See 2 Chronicles 1:7-12.)

Again moving on in history, Ezra recognized that the use of weapons by those who rely upon God would be shameful. By the river Ahava, Ezra proclaimed a fast so that his followers would humble themselves before God and pray to Him for successful journey. He told them he was "ashamed to ask the king for an armed guard and cavalry to protect us from an enemy on the road, for we had already told the king, 'The hand of our God is held out in blessing over all who seek him, his power and his anger over all who turn away from Him' " (Ezra 8:22, 23). Ezra taught that he who relies on God has no need for weapons.

The writer of the psalms told us that "a large army will not keep a king safe, nor does the hero escape by his great strength; it is delusion to rely on the horse for safety, for all its power, it cannot save. But see how the eye of Yahweh is on those who fear him, on those who rely on his love, to rescue their souls from death and keep them alive in famine" (Ps. 33:16-19). And later the psalmist said, "The strength of the war horse means nothing to him, it is not infantry that interests him. Yahweh is interested only in those who fear him, in those who rely on his love" (Ps. 147: 10, 11).

The writer of Proverbs, anticipating the Sermon on the Mount, taught, "Do not say, " 'I will repay evil': put your hope in Yahweh and he will keep you safe. . . . Do not say, 'I will treat him as he has treated me; I will repay each man as he deserves.' . . . "If you enemy is hungry, give him something to eat; if thirsty, something to drink. By this you heap red-hot coals on his head, and Yahweh will reward you" (Prov. 20:22; 24:29; 25:21).

The Book of Wisdom anticipating Paul, stated:

> For armor he will take his jealous love,
> he will arm creation to punish his enemies;

he will put on justice as a breastplate,
and for helmet wear his undissembling judgment;
he will take up invincible holiness for shield,
he will forge a biting sword of his stern wrath,
and the universe will march with him to fight the reckless.
Bolts truly aimed, the shafts of lightning will leap,
and from the clouds, as from a full-drawn bow, fly to their mark;
and the catapult will hurl hailstones charged with fury.
The waters of the sea will rage against them,
the rivers engulf them without pity.
The breath of Omnipotence will blow against them
and winnow them like a hurricane.
So lawlessness will bring the whole earth to ruin
and evil-doing bring the thrones of the mighty down. . . .
Wielding the weapons of his sacred office,
prayer and atoning incense,
he took his stand against the Anger and put an end to the calamity,
showing that he was indeed your servant.
He conquered the bitter plague, not by physical strength,
not by force of arms;
but by word he prevailed over the Punisher (Wisdom 5:17-24; 18:21, 22).

The Lord has taught that vengeance is His, not ours. When the Old Testament talks about violence, war, and vengeance, it is God's doing, not man's. When man makes war and violence, he usurps the power of his Creator and attempts to become a god unto himself. What is the result? A humanity torn with violence and terror!

Toward the end of the Old Testament we find the familiar phrase of Micah which gives us a glimpse of the messianic age:

He will wield authority over many peoples
and arbitrate for mighty nations;
they will hammer their swords into plowshares,
their spears into sickles.

> Nations will not lift sword against nation,
> there will be no more training for war.
> Each man will sit under his vine and his fig tree,
> with no one to trouble him.
> The mouth of Yahweh Sabaoth has spoken it (Mic. 4:3, 4).

Zechariah bluntly said, "The bow of war will be banished" (Zech. 9:10).

These are but samplings of numerous statements, prophecies, writings, lamentations, and proverbs in the Old Testament indicating that violence is not permanent, not the way of God, not the way of His people, and soon through the suffering of God's Servant will be no more. This was not to say that violence would end but that God's children would no longer do violence.

I have intentionally left the writings of Isaiah to the end of this discourse for there we find the main connecting thread between the old and the new, the message of the New Testament heralded by the Old — the prophecy of the Suffering Servant.

Vernard Eller in his *King Jesus, Manual of Arms for the 'Armless*[2] writes beautifully on this thesis. He expands upon the relationship of Isaiah's prophecy of the Suffering Servant to the New Testament teachings of Jesus and Christian nonviolence. Isaiah the prophet said:

> All the boots of trampling soldiers
> and the garments fouled with blood
> shall become a burning mass, fuel for fire.
> For a boy has been born for us, a son given to us
> to bear the symbol of dominion on his shoulder;
> and he shall be called
> in purpose wonderful, in battle God-like,
> Father for all time, Prince of peace (Is. 9:5-7; NEB).

And so for those who will not rely on the Prince of Peace:

> Woe to those who go down to Egypt
> to seek help there,

who build their hopes on cavalry,
who rely on the number of chariots
and on the strength of mounted men,
but never look to the Holy One of Israel
nor consult Yahweh (Is. 31:1).

Eller correctly views Isaiah as predicting a Messiah who is neither warrior nor judge but servant — pacifistic, non-resistant, and loving. There can be no just war for the followers of this Messiah.

Eller comments, "So Isaiah is saying, in effect, that there is no such thing as a just war because there are no peoples who themselves are just enough to fight them. The motives of even the best of peoples are impure and sinful enough that any wars they fight are bound to be sinful, too.[3] Israel desired to take over her own defense as an aspect or defiance of God. "Isaiah explicitly brands Israel's military preparedness — her arms and alliances and whatever — as being part of her sin, as a particular sign of her failure to trust in Yahweh and His promise for Zion and mankind."[4] Eller sees Isaiah describing the "fighting" of the Suffering Servant as the exact reverse of what we normally consider fighting to be. "Instead of power, the Servant displays weakness; instead of glory, humiliation; instead of public acclaim, social rejection; instead of assertive thrust against the enemy, absorption of the enemies' thrust against Him; instead of making the enemy suffer, suffering Himself. Although it will be difficult for us to understand it so, this is a means by which God truly does win the victory and achieve His will.[5]

Isaiah explains how this reverse fighting works:

Yet on himself he bore our sufferings,
  our torments he endured,
 while we counted him smitten by God,
  struck down by disease and misery;

but he was pierced for our transgressions,
tortured for our iniquities;
the chastisement he bore is health for us
and by his scourging we are healed.
We had all strayed like sheep,
each of us had gone his own way;
but the LORD laid upon him
the guilt of us all.
He was afflicted, he submitted to be struck down
and did not open his mouth;
he was led like a sheep to the slaughter,
like a ewe that is dumb before the shearers.
Without protection, without justice, he was taken away;
and who gave a thought to his fate,
how he was cut off from the world of living men,
stricken to the death for my people's transgression?
He was assigned a grave with the wicked,
a burial-place among the refuse of mankind,
though he had done no violence
and spoken no word of treachery.
Yet the Lord took thought for his tortured servant
and healed him who had made himself a sacrifice for sin;
so shall he enjoy long life and see his children's children,
and in his hand the lord's cause shall prosper.
After all his pains he shall be bathed in light,
after his disgrace he shall be fully vindicated;
so shall he, my servant, vindicate many,
himself bearing the penalty of their guilt.
Therefore I will allot him a portion with the great,
and he shall share the spoil with the mighty,
because he exposed himself to face death
and was reckoned among transgressors,
because he bore the sin of many
and interceded for their transgressions (Is. 53:4-12; NEB).

Eller concludes:

"Genesis showed us that wars and fightings come about because man decided to quit fighting along with Yahweh in

> a ballerina posture and instead fight it in his own way and for his own end, which is the construction of security for himself. Joshua-Judges taught us that the only cure is for man to make the determined and disciplined effort to join Yahweh in His war and let Him call the shots. It went on to portray a sincere and honest effort at doing this — which effort, even so, was destined to fall short. Isaiah spoke to that failure by pointing out that man has so perverted himself that his ways of fighting simply are incapable of serving God's battle plan. And finally, Duetero came in to tell us that God's method of fighting is different from what we have been considering and thus opens again the possibility that man might have a role to play after all.[6]

The prophets of the Old Testament predict the end of violence coming with the new age. The Old Testament begins with murder, proceeds to the law of an eye for an eye and a tooth for a tooth, and reaches its zenith in the prophecy of the Suffering Servant. The Old Testament indeed is a prophecy of the Christian nonviolence of the messianic era, an era marked by nonresistance and peacemaking. Unfortunately at some point later in time. Christian leaders took a vast step backward and rejoined the judges of the law and the kings of war, left the teachings of Isaiah and Jesus, and returned to the *Lex Talionis* and Holy War of the Old Testament. Only a remnant remains now who follow King Jesus. Today Christians who follow "King" Constantine are in essence imitating those in Christ's day who said, "We have no king but Caesar." But in the days of the apostles, Christians knew better.

Part II

The Spirit and the Power: *The Authority of Caesar*

CHAPTER 4

Apostolic Witnesses of the Peace Gospel

Following Pentecost, the apostles remembered and understood the teachings of Christ's message of peace. They know it was the hallmark of the entire message of love. Killing and violence, hate and anger grieved the Spirit and exhalted the evil one. Paul said to the Ephesians:

> Finally, grow strong in the Lord, with the strength of his power. Put God's armor on so as to be able to resist the devil's tactics. For it is not against human enemies that we have to struggle, but against the Sovereignties and the Powers who originate the darkness in this world, the spiritual army of evil in the heavens. That is why you must rely on God's armor, or you will not be able to put up any resistance when the worst happens, or have enough resources to hold your ground.

> So stand your ground, with truth buckled around your waist, and integrity for a breastplate, wearing for shoes on your feet the eagerness to spread the gospel of peace and always carrying the shield of faith so that you can use it to put out the burning arrows of the evil one. And then you must accept salvation from God to be your helmet and receive the Word of God from the Spirit to use as a sword. (Eph. 6:10-17).

So Paul, who formerly murdered Christians in "righteous anger," was reborn through Jesus. He stopped killing and started loving. The violent Saul became the nonviolent Paul. Acts 7:55-60 tells us Saul stood by as "Stephen, filled with the Holy Spirit, gazed into heaven and saw the glory of God, and Jesus standing at God's right hand." The members of the council shouted at Stephen. They rushed at him, stoned him, forced him out of the city. As they were stoning him, Stephen said, "Lord Jesus, receive my spirit." And he knelt down and said aloud, "Lord do not hold this sin against them." And with these words he "fell asleep." Stephen was practicing Christian nonresistance. Saul entirely approved the killing. For Saul, this violence was just. If ever there was a man who believed in the just violence theory, it was Saul of Tarsus. And if ever there was a man who was converted to the nonviolence of Christianity, it was Paul the apostle. But for the forgiveness of Stephen, one wonders if there ever would have been a Paul.

In Romans Paul, speaking of non-Christians of the time, said:

> Their feet are swift when blood is to be shed,
> wherever they go there is havoc and ruin.
> They know nothing of the way of peace,
> there is no fear of God before their eyes (Rom. 3:15-18).

And later in his same letter speaking to Christians, he said:

> Bless those who persecute you: never curse them, bless them. Rejoice with those who rejoice and be sad with those in sorrow. Treat everyone with equal kindness; never be condescending but make real friends with the poor. Do not allow yourself to become self-satisfied. Never repay evil with evil but let everyone see that you are interested only in the highest ideals. Do all you can to live at peace with everyone. Never try to get revenge; leave that, my friends, to God's anger. As scripture says: Vengeance is mine — I will pay them back, the Lord promises. But there is more: If your enemy is hungry, you should give him food, and if he is thirsty, let him drink. Thus you heap red-hot coals on his head. Resist evil and conquer it with good. . . . Love is the one thing that cannot hurt your neighbor; that is why it is the answer to every one of the commandments (Rom. 12:14-21; 13:10).

Paul in 1 Corinthians tells us how it was with his Christians:

> Here we are, fools for the sake of Christ, while you are the learned men in Christ; we have no power, but you are influential; you are celebrities, we are nobodies. To this day, we go without food and drink and clothes; we are beaten and have no homes; we work for our living with our own hands. When we are cursed, we answer with a blessing; when we are hounded, we put up with it; we are insulted and we answer politely. We are treated as the offal of the world, still to this day, the scum of the earth (1 Cor. 4:10-13).

Does that sound like the Christian of today? Or does Paul's description of non-Christians have a more familiar ring?

And if it were not obvious from Paul's conversion that Christians should abhor violence, Paul made it abundantly clear in 2 Corinthians 10:3-5 when he said, "We live in the flesh, of course, but the muscles that we fight with are not flesh. Our war is not fought with weapons of flesh, yet they are strong enough, in God's cause, to demolish fortresses."

The disciples, far from advocating war, taught us exactly what war is and why we should avoid it. James said:

> Where do these wars and battles between yourselves first start? Isn't it precisely in the desires fighting inside your own selves? You want something and you haven't got it; so you are prepared to kill. You have an ambition that you cannot satisfy; so you fight to get your way by force. Why you don't have what you want is because you don't pray for it; when you do pray and don't get it, it is because you have not prayed properly, you have prayed for something to indulge your own desires. (Jas. 4:1-3).

He talked of those of us who have caused the violence in this world and done the killing both physically and psychologically. He made reference to those who offer no resistance, who practice Christian nonviolence, when he spoke to the rich and said:

> Now an answer for the rich. Start crying, weep for the miseries that are coming to you. Your wealth is all rotting, your clothes are all eaten up by moths. All your gold and your silver are corroding away, and the same corrosion will be your own sentence, and eat into your body. It was a burning fire that you stored up as your treasure for the last days. Laborers mowed your fields, and you cheated them — listen to the wages that you kept back, calling out; realize that the cries of the reapers have reached the ears of the Lord of hosts. On earth you have had a life of comfort and luxury; in the time of slaughter you went on eating to your heart's content. It was you who condemned the innocent and killed them; they offered you no resistance (Jas. 5:1-6).

On the other hand James said: "Peacemakers, when they work for peace, sow the seeds which will bear fruit in holiness" (Jas. 3:18).

How clear the message must have been in those times. Peter said:

> This, in fact, is what you were called to do, because Christ suffered for you and left an example for you to follow the

> way he took. He had not done anything wrong, and there had been no perjury in his mouth. He was insulted and did not retaliate with insults; when he was tortured he made no threats but he put his trust in the righteous judge. He was bearing our faults in his own body on the cross, so that we might die to our faults and live for holiness; through his wounds you have been healed. You had gone astray like sheep but now you have come back to the shepherd and guardian of your souls. (1 Pet. 2:21-25).

We too have gone astray like sheep and hopefully are now coming back also. "Anyone who claims to be in the light but hates his brother is still in the dark" (1 Jn. 2:9). Are we in the light or the dark?

The ideal of the Sermon on the Mount was practiced by the apostles. They were mostly martyrs. They followed in the footsteps of Jesus. They advocated no involvement with the government except that Christians were not to resist it violently. Jesus told them, "Peace I bequeath to you, my own peace I give you, a peace the world cannot give, this is my gift to you" (Jn. 14:27). They had the peace of the Spirit. They did not make war, they did not use violence, and they spread the gospel and its lifestyle throughout the Mediterranean. Paul says, "How beautiful are the feet of them that preach the gospel of peace" (Rom. 10:15, KJV). "So stand your ground . . . wearing for shoes on your feet the eagerness to spread the gospel of peace" (Eph. 6:14, 15). And so on and on the admonitions of the apostles regarding peace unfold in the New Testament under the guidance of the Holy Spirit.

But the apostles died, many as martyrs. Would the gospel of peace be transmitted faithfully from one man to another — not necessarily a man with the title "apostle" or "disciple" but perhaps a businessman, a teacher, a merchant? What would happen? The apostles were gone by the second century. But many followers lived on who were taught by them, or who had been in the company of the apostles and of Jesus.

Until approximately AD 170, or a lifetime after the death of the last apostle, there is no record of any Christian waging war. After that time the issue of pacifism and militarism began to emerge when some Christians, forgetting the commandment of love and the power of nonresistance, took up the sword. Then every leading spokesman of the church for the next 150 years, proclaimed the gospel of peace in essentially the same language and lifestyle as the apostles had taught. Aristides, Justin Martyr, Athenagoras, Tatian, Clement of Rome, Clement of Alexandria, Irenaeus, Tertullian, Origen, Hyppolytus, Minucius, Cyprian, Maximilian, Arnobius, Lactantius, Martin of Tours, as well as the church disciplines and regulations of the time — the *Didache*, the *Didaskalia*, the Testament of our Lord, and Egyptian church order — all proclaimed the lifestyle of peace enunciated by the apostles.

Twelve men went out into the world, ignorant and unlettered, but by the power of God they proclaimed Christ's message of love. The early Christians practiced it.

CHAPTER 5

The Early Christian Peacemakers

Following the apostles, the early Christians witnessed to the peace gospel of Jesus for over 300 years. Many of them lived the lifestyle of the gospel, and their statements are recorded in history. Some of these statements are offered here in memory of those whom we so often have forgotten or didn't even know. We tend to skip from Paul to Augustine in our reading without stopping to contemplate the writings of those between who were also dedicated followers of Christ. A chronological reading of these writings dating from the second, third, and fourth centuries establishes clearly that the first Christians interpreted the teachings of Jesus as a call for a life of pacifism and nonresistance.

Nonresistance and pacifism were key words in their discipleship. The idea of nonresistance was taken from the teaching of Jesus to offer the wicked man no resistance, and pacifism from His words: "Blessed are the peacemakers." The Latin word for peacemakers is *pacifici*. A combination of the negative command of nonresistance, the affirmative command of love, and the occupation of peacemaking constituted early Christian nonviolence. Consider the following examples of Christian teachings on nonviolence in the centuries immediately following Christ.

The Didache (c. 100)

The *Didache* or "the Teaching of the Twelve Apostles" is thought to be the earliest handbook of church rules. Its author is unknown. The original name for the practice of Christianity was "The Way." The *Didache* said:

> 1. There are two Ways, one of Life and one of Death, and there is a great difference between the two Ways.
>
> 2. The Way of Life is this: "First, thou shalt love the God who made thee, secondly, thy neighbour as thyself; and whatsoever thou wouldst not have done to thyself, do not thou to another."
>
> 3. Now, the teaching of these words is this: "Bless those that curse you, and pray for your enemies, and fast for those that persecute you. For what credit is it to you if you love those that love you? Do not even the heathen do the same?" But, for your part, "love those that hate you," and you will have no enemy.
>
> 4. "Abstain from carnal and bodily "lusts." If any man smite thee on the right cheek, turn to him the other cheek also," and thou wilt be perfect. "If any man impress thee to go with him one mile, go with him two. If any man take thy coat, give him thy shirt also. If any man will take from thee what is thine, refuse it not" — not even if thou canst.
>
> 5. Give to everyone that asks thee, and do not refuse, for the Father's will is that we give to all from the gifts we have received.[1]

Aristides (c. 125)

Aristides defended Christianity before the Roman emperor, Hadrian. He was a pacifistic witness of the second century.[2] Described as a man of faith, devoted to the Christian religion, and a philosopher of Athens, he wrote an apology in which he described as Christian those who "comfort their oppressors and do good to their enemies . . . love one another."[3]

Justin Martyr (c. 130)

Justin Martyr, a Greek born in Samaria about AD 100, taught in Rome and established what might be thought of as the first Christian school. Justin declared that Christians will gladly die for Christ's sake: "We refrain from making war on our enemies . . . for Caesar's soldiers possess nothing which they can lose more precious than their life, while our love goes out to that eternal life which God will give us by His might."[4] He said, "We who were filled with war, and mutual slaughter, and every wickedness, have each of us through the whole earth changed our warlike weapons — our swords into plowshares and our spears into the implements of tillage."[5] At another place he writes. "We who formerly murdered one another now not only do not make war upon our enemies, but that we may not lie or deceive our judges, we gladly die confessing Christ."[6]

In his *Dialogue* he quotes Micah 4:3 as finding its fulfillment in Christianity: "They will hammer their swords into plowshares . . ."[7] Justin was martyred in approximately AD 165.

Tatian (c. 150)

Tatian was another of the early pacifists of the second century.[8] In the third century Syrian Christianity "already had its solitaries dedicated to chastity and abstinence from wine and flesh. In such circles we find also a rejection of military service. Tatian, as early as the second century, was a forerunner. His provenance is commonly thought to have been Mesopotamia. He was an ascetic and a founder of the Encratites. Military service appears in a list of his aversions: 'I have no desire to rule. I crave not riches. I decline military command. I hate fornication.' "[9]

However, he paid the tribute ordered by the emperor in imitation of Christ.[10]

Clement of Rome (c. 150)

Clement was a bishop of Rome at the beginning of the second century, listed by some authorities as the third Roman bishop after Peter. Two letters were proported to have been authored by him some fifty years apart. The second says this:

> 1. Wherefore, brethren, let us forsake our sojourning in this world, and do the will of Him who called us, and let us not fear to go forth from this world. 2. for the Lord said, "Ye shall be as lambs in the midst of wolves." 3. and Peter answered and said to him, "If then the wolves tear the lambs?" 4. Jesus said to Peter, "Let the lambs have no fear of the wolves after their death; and do ye have no fear of those that slay you, and can do nothing more to you, but fear him who after your death hath power over body and soul, to cast them into the flames of hell." 5. And be well assured, brethren, that our sojourning in this world in the flesh is a little thing and lasts a short time, but the promise of Christ is great and wonderful, and brings us rest, in the kingdom which is to come and in everlasting life.[11]

Athenagoras (c. 175)

Athenagoras, a Christian layman of Athens, was considered the most eloquent of the Greek Christian philosophers. He said:

> Christians cannot bear to see a man put to death, even justly.[12]
>
> We have learnt not only not to strike back and not to go to law with those who plunder and rob us, but with some if they buffet us on the side of the head, to offer the other side of the head to them for a blow, and with others if they take away our tunic to give them also our cloak.[13]
>
> For it is not enough to be just (and justice is to return like for like), but it is incumbent on us to be good and patient of evil. . . . For when they know that we cannot endure even to see a man put to death, though justly, who of them can accuse us of murder or cannibalism? . . . And when we say that those women who use drugs to bring on abortion commit murder, and will have to give an account to God for the abortion, on what principle should we commit murder?[14]

The Didaskalia (c. 180)

Stanley Windass writes of the *Didaskalia* that these early church rules "still forbade the receipt of money from magistrates polluted by war, and abstination from the blood of animals remained the general rule; but it became even more clear for the Christians than for the Jews that the murder of Abel by Cain was indeed the archtypical crime, the pattern of all human crime and bloodshed. The sin of murder was regarded with the utmost horror, and murderers were permanently excluded from the Christian community."[15]

Clement of Alexandria (c. 180)

Clement, who lived between AD 150 and 215, was the head of the catechetical school in Alexandria at the center of Hellenistic culture. According to Windass,

> It is impossible to appreciate the attitude of the early church toward war unless we can recapture something of its vision; and since it is a vision which can only be recaptured in poetry, it is to the actual words of the early Fathers that we

should go. Nothing exemplifies the vision more splendidly than a little poem of Clement of Alexandria:

Now the trumpet sounds with a mighty voice, calling
the soldiers of the world to arms, announcing war;
And shall not Christ, who has uttered His summons
to peace even to the ends of the earth,
Summon together His own soldiers of peace?
Indeed, O Man, He has called to arms with His blood
and His word an army that sheds no blood;
To these soldiers He has handed over the kingdom
of heaven.
The trumpet of Christ is His gospel. He has sounded
it in our ears and we have heard it.
Let us be armed for peace, putting on the armor
of justice, seizing the shield of faith,
The helmet of salvation,
And sharpening the sword of the spirit which is the
word of God.
This is how the apostle prepares us peacefully for
battle.
Such are the arms that make us invulnerable.
So armed, let us prepare to fight the evil one.
Let us cut through his flaming attack with the blade
which the Logos Himself has tempered in the waters
of baptism.
Let us reply to His goodness by praise and thanksgiving.
"While thou art yet speaking," He says, "Here I am."[16]

Clement also said, "Above all, Christians are not allowed to correct by violence sinful wrongdoings. For it is not those who abstain by choice that God crowns. For it is not possible for a man to be good steadily except by his own choice."[17] And further:

> In peace not in war we are trained. War needs great preparation, but peace and love, quiet sisters, require no arms, no expensive outlay. Various peoples incite the passions of war by martial music; Christians employ only the Word of God, the instrument of peace. . . .[18]

He said to the heathen,

> "If you enroll as one of God's people, heaven is your country and God your lawgiver. And what are His laws? . . . Thou shalt not kill. . . . Thou shalt love thy neighbor as thyself. To him that strikes thee on the one cheek, turn also the other."[19]

Irenaeus (c. 185)

Irenaeus was a disciple of Polycarp of Smyrna, John the Apostle's disciple. Irenaeus lived between AD 130 and 200 and, although born in Asia Minor, became Bishop of Lyons, France. Interestingly, his name derives from the Greek *eirené* (peace).

Irenaeus commenting on the early followers of Christ who, when struck, merely offered the other cheek said, "If He Himself did not in reality suffer before us, He will seem to have led us astray when He exhorted us to be beaten and to turn the other cheek."[20]

> . . . As to the union, harmony, and peace among the various animals which are by nature mutually inimical and hostile, the elders say that it will really be so, when Christ comes again to be King over all. In this way there is indicated as if by a parable the gathering together of men of various and different nations in peace and harmony in the name of Christ . . . and this has already happened: for those who before were quite perverse and who let no evil work undone, now that they have come to know and to believe in Christ and as soon as they have embraced the faith, have changed their manner of living, and they adhere to the severest demands of righteousness.[21]

He several times refers to the prohibition of killing and quotes Micah and Isaiah on beating our swords into plowshares.[22]

Tertullian (c. 200)

Tertullian (AD 160-220), a native of Carthage, was a lawyer and the first Christian theologian to write in Latin. He wrote, "Those whom the Christian has put to flight in the daytime by exorcisms, shall he defend them by night, leaning and resting on the lance with which Christ's side was pierced? And shall he carry a flag too that is rival to Christ's?"[23] And also, "Shall he apply the chain, and the prison, and the torture, and the punishment, who is not the avenger of his own wrongs."[24]

In Tertullian's time, Old Testament precedent was already being quoted in support of the theory that Christians must bear arms.[25] He goes out of his way to explain that the military characters used in Scripture are simply figurative.[26] "The military oath and the baptismal vow are inconsistent with each other the one being the sign of Christ, the other of the devil."[27] He was an extreme antimilitarist, and to some of his pagan critics who accused Christians of the crime of nonresistance he replied, "Shall it be held lawful to make an occupation of the sword, when the Lord proclaimed that he who takes the sword shall also perish by the sword? And shall the Son of Peace take part in battle when it does not become him even to sue in law?"[28] And further, "How shall a Christian man wage war, nay, how shall he even be a soldier in peacetime, without the sword, which the Lord has taken away?'[29] Tertullian confirmed that upon conversion many Christians withdrew from military service.[30] "Christ in disarming Peter ungirt every soldier."[31] Tertullian obviously regarded war as organized sin. He declared that Christians would rather be killed than kill.[32]

Tertullian refutes those who say that John, Peter, and Jesus did not influence the centurions whom they met to abandon their arms.[33] He says to Emperor Verus: "Not a

Christian could be found in any of the rebel armies"[34] nor could they fight against Rome.

Origen (c. 225)

Origen (185-254), the son of a martyr who was tortured and killed in 213 for his beliefs, was head of the Christian school in Alexandria before his exile to Palestine. Commenting on the words of Christ to Peter in the Garden of Gethsemane, "He who takes the sword shall perish by the sword," Origen taught that Christ wanted us to put away the warlike sword, and to take the sword of the Spirit; and that we must beware lest "for warfare, or for the vindication of our rights, or for any occasion, we should take out the sword, for no such occasion is allowed by this evangelical teaching."[36]

Origen said about Christians that "no longer do we take the sword against any nations nor do we learn war anymore since we have become the sons of peace, for the sake of Jesus who is our leader."[37] He said Christians need not fight for their kings.

Origen was raised to priesthood by a bishop, but eventually was martyred. He died four years after imprisonment and torture in the Decian persecution. He said of Jesus: "He nowhere teaches that it is right for His own disciples to offer violence to anyone, however wicked. For He did not deem it in keeping with such laws as His, which were derived from a divine source, to allow the killing of any individual whatever."[38] Hc proclaimed that "none fight better for the king than we do. We do not indeed fight under him, although he require it, but we fight on his behalf, forming a special army, an army of piety, by offering our prayers to God."[39] Origen took for granted that the Christian is a peacemaker and "does not indulge in warfare,"[40] not even in defense of family. "We who by our prayers destroy all demons which stir up wars, violate oaths, and disturb the peace, are of more help to the emperors than those who seem to be doing the fighting."[41]

Hippolytus (c. 225)

Hippolytus was elected bishop and therefore Pope of Rome in AD 217 during Pope Callistus' reign. After years of conflict between these two popes, both resigned as friends, and a new pope was elected. Windass writes of the Canons of Hippolytus (also known as "Apostolic Tradition"):

> Hippolytus was a Roman churchman, who drew up a list of rules for all matters of church discipline, some time in the first part of the third century. His "canons," as they came to be called, are a mine of information for the traditions of the period at which he writes, and he is on the whole very conservative and very accurate. The main purpose of his work, as he says himself, is to defend the traditional practices of the church against the recent error and apostasy of ignorant men. Two of his canons concern the question of military service; and, in spite of the obscurity of later versions, there is very little doubt about what these two canons originally conveyed. One said that a man could not be received as a Christian if he was in the army of the emperor; and the other said that a catechumen who showed military ambitions was to be rejected because "(this) is far from the Lord."[42]

Ellul tells us that the "Apostolic Tradition" declared that he who holds the sword must cast it away and that if one of the faithful becomes a soldier, he must be rejected by the church "for he has scorned God."[43] Hippolytus admonished Christians that "a soldier of civil authority must be taught not to kill men and to refuse to do so if he is commanded."[44] Macgregor reports in *The New Testament Basis of Pacifism* that Hippolytus held that a soldier who confesses himself a Christian member is to be excluded from the sacraments until he has done penance for the blood which he has shed.[45]

Minucius Felix (c. 225)

Very little is known of Minucius Felix, a Latin apologist layman and lawyer born in Africa. He wrote: "It is not right for us either to see or hear a man being killed."[46]

Cyprian (c. 250)

Cyprian (AD 200-258), the primate of Carthage, was beheaded near Carthage in AD 258. He died protesting the dual standard of morality which holds that "if a murder is committed privately it is a crime, but if it happens with the state authority courage is the name for it"[47] Cyprian said, "The world is wet with mutual bloodshed; and homicide is a crime when individuals commit it [but] it is called a virtue when many commit it. Not the reason of innocence, but the magnitude of savagery insures inpunity for crimes."[48] And God willed iron to be for the culture of the earth, he said.[49] And further, "God . . . designed man for tilling, not for killing."[50]

Cyprian reminded his brethren of Paul's hymn of love, "And what more — that you should not curse; that you should not seek again your goods when taken from you; when buffeted you should turn the other cheek; and forgive not seven times but seventy times seven. . . . That you should love your enemies and pray for your adversaries and persecutors."[51]

Maximilian (c. 295)

Windass tells us: "A young African called Maximilian was summoned before the proconsul to serve in the army (he was the son of a veteran and was therefore one of the few who had an obligation to serve), but he refused simply on the grounds that he was a Christian and 'could not do evil.' He stuck to his point despite the persuasiveness of the proconsul who observed that there were new Christians in the army. As a result he was led away to execution."[52]

Maximilian said, "My arms are with the Lord, I cannot fight for any earthly consideration. I am now a Christian."[53] He died in 295, a martyr.[54]

Arnobius (c. 300)

Arnobius of Sicca, also known as Arnobius the Elder, was born a pagan and for a time was outspoken in his opposition to Christianity. As a result of a dream, he was converted.

O'Gara writes: "Arnobius was a foremost Christian apologist in Diocletian's time. He pitted Christ against the rulers of the Roman Empire and asked: 'Did He, claiming royal power for Himself, occupy the world with fierce legions, and, [of] nations at peace from the beginning, destroy and remove some, and compel others to put their necks beneath His yoke and obey Him? . . .' What use is it to the world that there should [be] . . . generals of the greatest experience in warfare, skilled in the capture of cities, and soldiers immovable [and] invincible in cavalry battles or in a fight on foot?"[55]

Arnobius, along with Tertullian, Menucius Felix, and Lactantius was one of the Latin apologists. He denied that God intended that men "should tear up and break down the rights of kinship, overturn their cities, devastate land in enmity, make slaves of free men, violate maidens and other men's wives, hate one another, envy the joys and good fortunes of others, in a word curse, carp at, and rend one another with the biting of savage teeth."[56]

Arnobius argued that the peace of the Pax Romana

resulted from the peaceableness of Christians: "For since we, a numerous band of men as we are, have learned from His teaching and His laws that evil ought not to be requited with evil, that it is better to suffer wrong than to inflict it, that we should rather shed our own blood than stain our hands and our conscience with that of another, an ungrateful world is now for a long period enjoying a benefit from Christ, inasmuch as by His means the rage of savage ferocity has been softened, and has begun to withhold hostile hands from the blood of a fellow-creature."[57]

Lactantius (c. 300)

Lactantius (AD 240-320), a pupil of Arnobius, was born in Africa and as a pagan taught rhetoric to Diocletian, the Roman Emperor. Upon becoming a Christian he was required to resign his teaching position. Pope John XXIII referred to him in *Pacem in Terris*.[58] Lactantius, writing at the end of the second century, said, "Man is so sacrosanct a creature that it is always wrong to kill him. . . . No exception can be made to this commandment of God."[59]

He wrote further, "When God forbids us to kill, He not only prohibits us from open violence, which is not even allowed by public laws, but He warns us against the commission of those things which are esteemed lawful among men. Thus, it can never be lawful for a righteous man to go to war, since his warfare is in righteousness itself: nor to accuse anyone of a capital charge, since it makes no difference whether you put a man to death by word or by sword, since it is the act of putting to death which is prohibited. Therefore, with regard to this precept of God, there can be no exception at all. . . . It is always unlawful to put a man to death."[60]

In another place he writes, "Truly the more men that have afflicted, despoiled, (and) slain, the more noble and renowned do they think themselves; and, captured by the appearance of empty glory, they give the name of excellence to their crimes. Now I would rather that they should make gods of themselves from the slaughter of wild beasts than that they should approve of an immorality so bloody. If anyone has slain a single man, he is regarded as contaminated and wicked, nor do they think it right that he should be admitted to the earthly dwelling of the gods. But he who has slaughtered endless thousands of men, deluged the fields with blood, (and) infected rivers (with it) is admitted not only to a temple, but even to heaven."[61]

Says MacGregor: "These statements will appear all the more striking if we remember that they were made by men for whom the Old Testament, with its frequent glorification of nationalism and militarism, was the Word of God in as full a sense as the New."[62]

Martin, Bishop of Tours (c. 335)

Martin was born of pagan parents in Hungary, and his father was a military tribune. When he was ten years old Martin became a catechumen. At fifteen he entered the Roman army, with misgivings. He was baptized and two years later left the army for reasons of conscience. Severus wrote about Martin's retirement from military service: "For Christ did not require to secure any other victory on behalf of His own soldiers than that the enemy be subdued without bloodshed, no one should suffer death."[63] Martin exclaimed on his refusal to serve any longer in the army, "If this conduct of mine is ascribed to cowardice, not to faith, I will take my stand unarmed before the line of battle tomorrow, and in the name of the Lord Jesus, protected by the sign of the cross, and not by shield or helmet, I will safely penetrate the ranks of the enemy." He was sent to prison, but on the following day, the enemy sent ambassadors who surrendered both themselves and all their possessions.[64]

Other Witnesses

In 1845 George Beckwith, a peace advocate of the nineteenth century, wrote on the witness of the early Christians against war. He tells us that "Archeleaus, Ambrose, Chrysostom, Jerome, and Cyril . . . were of the opinion, that it is unlawful for Christians to engage in war."[65] Although other writings of Ambrose and Chrysostom indicate that they were not totally nonviolent, Chrysostom wrote in his Homilies: "Ought we not to resist an evil? Indeed we ought, but not by retaliation. (For) Christ hath commanded us to give up ourselves to suffering wrong freely, for thus shall we prevail over evil. For fire is not quenched by another fire, but by water."[66]

Beckwith continues: "We are told, also by Archeleaus, that many Roman soldiers who had embraced Christianity after having witnessed the piety and generosity of Marcellus, immediately forsook the profession of arms. We are told, also by Eusebius, that about the same time numbers laid aside a military life, and became private persons rather than abjure their religion."[67] Beckwith reports that Theophilus, Antiochenus, and Menucius Felix agreed. And he reports that Marinus was killed like Maximilian because he would not sacrifice to the Roman gods while in the army.[68] He reports that Tarachus said, "Because I am a Christian I have abandoned my profession as a soldier."[69]

Beckwith cites three basic instincts of these early Christians: (1) love of enemy, (2) abstention from violence, and (3) the conviction that slaughter of men in war was neither more nor less than direct murder. "The unlawfulness of fighting was as much a principle of religion in the early times of Christianity, as a refusal of sacrifice to the heathen gods. . . . Not until Christianity became corrupted did its followers become soldiers."[70]

Beckwith succinctly summarizes the Christian message of the early Christians as follows:

> Conclusion (1) that the early church fathers generally used language which obviously condemns all war, and not a few of them explicitly denounce it as utterly unchristian; (2) that they all speak of the ancient prophecies concerning the prevalence of peace under the gospel, as actually fulfilled in the Christians of that age; (3) that Christians then abstained from war as unlawful for them, and suffered martyrdom for their refusal to bear arms; (4) that ancient and modern infidels unite in ascribing to them these peculiar views; (5) that Celsus, near the close of the second century, charged them with refusing to bear arms under any circumstances, and Origen in his reply fifty years after, did not deny the charge, but justified them on the ground that Christianity forbids war; (6) that the war degeneracy of the church began very early in the third century, and went so far in the fourth that under and after Constantine the Great, Christians engaged in war, as they generally have ever since, with as little scruple as they did in any occupation of life.[71]

Among our own conclusions we would add the following: Anger, hatred, and killing were always condemned absolutely.[72] Bainton writes that all of the outstanding writers of the East and West repudiated participation in warfare for Christians.[73] No Christian took part in military service until approximately AD 170.[74] There was no participation in public affairs because such participation included pagan sacrifices, oaths, torture, and imprisonment.[75] The early believers did not go to law as a lawyer or a plaintiff, but only as a defendant. They did this because they were a new community.[76] They believed that nonviolence cannot fail against an enemy.[77]

Church regulations such as "The Testament of Our Lord" and "The Egyptian Church-Order" appeared about AD 430 but probably were in use much earlier. According to the former, a soldier could not be baptized unless he left the service and if a catechumen desired to be a soldier, he had either to give up the project or be excluded from the church.[78] The Egyptian Church Order simply ruled out altogether from church membership the magistrate who bears the sword.[79] Some scholars hold that the Egyptian Church Order, the Canons of Hippolytus, and the Apostolic Tradition are one and the same.

Following the example of Martin of Tours, Victricius, his friend and afterward Archbishop of Rouen, followed suit. The letter of Paulinus of Nola persuaded a friend to do the same. Basilius held that they who had shed blood in war should abstain from partaking in the sacrament of communion for three years.[80]

The Rise of Constantine

The peace witness of the early Christians began to crumble with the church's political marriage to Constantine in AD 311. The Synod of Arles in AD 314, called by the unbaptized Constantine, enacted a Canon opening military service to Christians.[81]

Tolstoy states that while the Council of Arles in AD 314 did open military service to Christians it also continued certian prohibitions:

> In the year 325, the first general council instituted a severe penance for Christians who went back to the army after having left it. Here are the exact terms of this order in the

> Russian translation, recognized by the Orthodox Church. "Called by grace to the profession of faith and having shown their first ardour in removing their warlike accoutrements, then having returned to them like dogs toward their vomitings . . . they should implore the Church for a period of ten years; asking pardon and listening to the Scriptures for three years on the threshold of the Church."
>
> Christians enrolled for the first time in the army were instructed not to kill their enemies during war. In the fourth century Basil the Great recommended that soldiers who had infringed this rule should not be admitted to the Communion for three years.
>
> One sees that the conviction that war is incompatible with Christianity was current not only during the first three centuries, during which time Christians were persecuted, but even at the moment of their triumph over paganism, when their doctrine was recognized as the State religion.
>
> Ferrucius declared it very clearly and paid for it with his life. He forbade Christians to shed blood, even in a just war and under the orders of Christian sovereigns. In the fourth century Lucifer, Bishop of Calaris, professed that the Christians should defend their greatest possession, faith, not in killing, but in sacrificing their own lives. Paulin, Bishop of Nole, who died in the year 431, threatened eternal torment to those who served Caesar bearing arms.[82]

In AD 325 it was Constantine who presided over the council of Nicea, not the pope. Its chief church architect, Athanasius, praised the just war in that year,[83] as did Ambrose in 400 and Augustine shortly thereafter. By AD 416 non-Christians were forbidden to serve in the army.[84]

Athanasius is the first of the early church theologians actually to praise war. He apparently did not object to the Emperor Constantine taking a strong hand on behalf of the Catholic Church against Arianism at Nicea. But several years later when the shoe was on the other foot and he was exiled five times over the Nicene-Arian controversy, he spoke against emperor rule in the church:

> If a decision was made by the bishops, what concern had the emperor with it? Or if it was but a threat of the emperor, what need then was there of the designated bishops? When in the world was such a thing ever before heard of? When did a decision of the Church receive its authority from the emperor? Or rather, when was his decree even recognized? There have been many councils in times past, and many decrees made by the Church; but never did the fathers seek the consent of the emperor for them, nor did the emperor busy himself in the affairs of the Church.
>
> The Apostle Paul had friends among those who belonged to the household of Caesar, and in writing to the Philippians he sent greetings from them: but never did he take them as associates in his judgments. But now we witness a novel spectacle, which is a discovery of the Arian heresy: heretics have assembled together with the Emperor Constantius, so that he, by alligning the authority of the bishops, may exercise his power against whomsoever he will, and while he persecutes may yet avoid the name of persecutor.[85]

Constantine removed the seat of Roman government to Byzantium and renamed the city in his own honor, Constantinople. He referred to it as the new Rome and to himself as a bishop outside the church. A feud between the cities arose which may have led Pope Damasus I in AD 382 to be the first to describe the church, which had been known only as the Catholic Church, as the Holy Roman Church. Henceforth the Holy Roman Catholic Church took on the trappings of the Roman Empire it was replacing.[86]

A Consistent Attitude Toward Violence

The aversion of early Christians to physical violence was not limited to war and capital punishment. Clement of Alexandria said: "For those women who conceal sexual wantoness by taking stimulating drugs to bring on an abortion wholly lose their humanity along with the fetus." Athanagoras wrote: "How could we kill a man — we who say that women who take drugs to procure abortion are guilty of homicide." On the same subject Tertullian stated: "There is no difference whether one snuffs out a life already born or disturbs one that is in the process of being born."[87]

Minucius Felix, Hippolytus, Cyprian, and Lactantius wrote similarly. Interestingly Ambrose and Augustine agreed and continued this tradition. The Roman Catholic Church has correctly emphasized that abortion is wrong as an act of unchristian violence. Unfortunately this church has not taken such a strong stand against war and capital punishment. On the other hand the historic peace churches have not been as certain about the violence of abortion as they have been about war and capital punishment.

For a short but glorious time, the impossible dream came true — Christians were known by the way they loved one another and their refusal to kill the unborn, the criminal, the enemy, or the aged for any reason. But that distant, peaceful Camelot too quickly came to an end except for a remnant.

CHAPTER 6

Kill for Justice?
The Birth of Christian Violence

Most Christians, particularly Roman Catholics, talk and act as if Christianity began with St. Augustine. Many do not read the Bible, and even those who can quote certain passages in the Old and New Testaments have no familiarity with the early church fathers, and therefore are not familiar with the theology of the first 300 years of Christ's church. A glance at one prominent Catholic treatise on the history of philosophy, for example, provides us with hundreds of pages of theological philosophy, but the thinking of the 300 years of the church on that subject is reduced to only fifteen pages.[1] This is representative of the emphasis given this period of the church by Catholic textbooks in the past.

More recently writers have provided us with an insight into what happened in that mysterious past which has heretofore been deemphasized. When Christ said to render to Caesar the things that are Caesar's and to God the things that are God's, this was not a licence for political government to require Christians to do other than what they should do toward their neighbor as Christians.

When Constantine the Great made Christianity the official religion of the empire early in the fourth century, the law and order of Rome became the basis for a new attitude toward peace and bloodshed. The voices of Athenagoras, Irenaeus, Tertullian, and the others were stilled by the teaching of Athanasius, Ambrose, and Augustine. Athanasius, a leading church authority at the Council of Nicea, supported certain forms of violence. He said: "Murder is not permitted, but to kill one's adversary in war is both lawful and praiseworthy."[2] What a change from what was taught earlier! Athanasius, the political whip of the Council of Nicea and chief sponsor of the Nicene legislation, joined with Constantine to perfect the marriage with Rome.

Augustine

At the time Athanasius was helping bring the church under Constantine's control, Augustine was not yet a Catholic. First a pagan and then a Manichaean, he came under the tutelage of Ambrose. By this time some Christians, unlike Maximilian, were serving in the army. Ambrose supported the just-war idea held by Athanasius and laid the base for such thinking in Augustine's mind.[3] Augustine became Bishop of Hippo and wrote from a position of close political involvement, for by this time the marriage of Christianity with Rome had been fifty years in the making.

The Roman Empire was attacked both in Europe and in Africa by the Vandals. Augustine was asked to reply to charges of disloyalty against Christians at this time of national threat. You may recall this question was raised before and answered by Origen. The Christians then claimed that they were not disloyal, but that prayer and witness were more effective than killing and murder. Was this Augustine's answer? No.

His answer, the most authoritative church statement of that time on the subject, was that an individual may serve the army and serve God as well.[4] We must not forget that shortly before this time, most Christians would not defend themselves, their religion, or their government with violence. Augustine broke with this rule in part. He said that a Christian may not defend himself because to kill in order to defend transitory things is obviously to show an undue attachment to them and therefore to commit sin. However, Augustine said that a man may be a Christian and a Roman soldier as well, and kill on behalf of the authority of the state. When he reached this conclusion the barbarians were at the gates of Hippo. He said, "Peace should be the object of your desire; war should be waged only as a necessity, and waged only that God may by it deliver men from the necessity and preserve them in peace. For peace is not sought in order to the kindling of war, but war is waged in order that peace may be attained. Therefore, even in waging war, cherish the spirit of a peacemaker, that by conquering those whom you attack, you may lead them back to the advantages of peace."[5]

In other writings Augustine carried forward a similar theme. In *Contra Faustus Manicheaeum* written in AD 397, Augustine presented his fullest statement on war. He said:

> What is the evil in war? Is it the death of some who will soon die in any case, that others may live in peaceful subjugation? This is mere cowardly dislike, not any religious feeling. The real evils in war are love of violence, revengeful cruelty, fierce and implacable enmity, wild resistance, and a lust of power, and such like; and it is generally to punish

> these things, when force is required to inflict the punishment, that, in obedience to God or some lawful authority, good men undertake wars, when they find themselves in such a position as regards the conduct of human affairs, that right conduct requires them to act or to make others act in this way. Otherwise John when the soldiers who came to be baptized asked, "What shall we do?" would have replied "Throw away your arms; give up the service, never strike, or wound, or disable anyone."
>
> But knowing that such actions in battle were not murderous, but authorized by law, and that the soldiers did not thus avenge themselves, but defend the public safety, he replied, "Do violence to no man, accuse no man falsely, and be content with your wages." But as the Manichaeans are in the habit of speaking evil of John, let them hear the Lord Jesus Christ Himself offering this money to be given to Caesar, which John tells the soldiers to be content with. "Give," he says, "to Caesar the things that are Caesar's." For tribute-money is given on purpose to pay the soldiers for war. Again, in the case of the centurion who said, "I am a man under authority, and have soldiers under me: and I say to one, 'Go,' and he goeth; and to another, 'Come,' and he cometh; and to my servant, 'Do this,' and he doeth it." Christ gave due praise to his faith; he did not tell him to leave the service. . . .[6]

Augustine thus abrogated all the early church fathers. He forgot or was unaware that Tertullian wrote: "The Testament of our Lord 'explained Christian teaching respecting soldiers: 'If anyone be a soldier or in authority, let him be taught not to oppress or to kill or to rob or be angry or to rage and afflict anyone.' "[7] And further, Tertullian said: "Of course, if faith comes later, and finds any preoccupied with military service, their case is different, as in the instance of those whom John used to receive for baptism, and of those most faithful centurions, I mean the centurion whom Christ approves, and the centurion whom Peter instructs;

yet, at the same time, when a man has become a believer, and faith has been sealed, there must be either an immediate abandonment of it, which has been the course with many; or all sorts of quibbling will have to be resorted to in order to avoid offending God."[8] This advice Marcellus, a centurion, followed and died for it.[9]

Nonetheless in a letter to another Marcellus, Augustine said, "For if the Christian religion condemned wars of every kind, the command given in the Gospel to soldiers taking counsel as to salvation would rather be to cast away their arms, and withdraw themselves wholly from military service; whereas the words spoken to such was, 'do violence to no man, neither accuse any falsely, and be content with your wages,' manifestly implying no prohibition to continue in the service."[10] This reasoning does not take into consideration that these words were spoken by John the Baptist not Jesus.

In his letter to Boniface, Augustine slipped back into Old Testament theology, cited the old wineskins, and applied the old law when he said: "Do not think that it is impossible for anyone to please God while engaged in active military service. Among such persons was the holy David, whom God gave so great a testimony; among them also were many righteous men of that time."[11]

Augustine said further:

> But, say they, the wise man will wage wars. As if he would not all the rather lament the necessity of just wars, if he remembers that he is a man; for if they were not just he would not wage them, and would therefore be delivered from all wars. For it is the wrong-doing of the opposing party which compels the wise man to wage just wars; and this wrong doing, even though it gave rise to no war, would still be matter of grief to man, because it is man's wrong-doing. Let every one, then, who thinks with pain on all these

> great evils, so horrible, so ruthless, acknowledge that this is misery. And if anyone either endures or thinks of them without mental pain, this is a more miserable plight still, for he thinks himself happy because he has lost human feeling.[12]

And further:

> Whoever gives even moderate attention to human affairs and to our common nature, will recognize that there is no man who does not wish to be joyful, neither is there anyone who does not wish to have peace. For even they who make wars desire nothing but victory — desire, that is to say, to attain to peace with glory. For what else is victory than the conquest of those who resist us, and when this is done there is peace. It is therefore with the desire for peace that wars are waged, even by those who take pleasure in exercising their war-like nature in command in battle. And hence, it is obvious that peace is the end sought for by war. For every man seeks peace by waging war, but no man seeks war by making peace. For even they who intentionally interrupt the peace in which they are living have no hatred to peace, but only wish it changed into a peace that suits them better. They do not, therefore, wish to have no peace, but only one more to their mind.[13]

Augustine justified conquering those who resist us whereas Jesus told us not to resist the evildoer. Finally Augustine said, "And thus we may say of peace, as we have said of eternal life, that it is the end of our good . . ."[14] Augustine missed the essential point of the peace gospel. Peace is not only an end. If we use violence as a means, we will never achieve peace. Peace must be the means as well as the end as the Sermon on the Mount teaches us.

O'Gara says, "To Augustine a war of defense was obviously justifiable, perhaps even obligatory. A war of aggression could be just if it were carried out with a proper authority and with both a just cause and a right intention.

The purpose of war was always to seek peace; war should only be fought if it is really necessary, and should be fought with mercy."[15]

But Windass asks, "How can one love one's enemies and also do them violence? How can one suffer injury gladly and at the same time retaliate? forgive injuries and at the same time punish the offender? In other words, the whole question of fitting the Sermon on the Mount into the scheme of the just war arises."[16]

Apparently, not all Catholics perceive the problem this lucidly. Thomas Merton said in an Introduction to the *City of God:* "St. Augustine's view of history is the view held by the Catholic Church , and by her Catholic tradition since the Apostles. It is a history of theology based on revelation."[17]

Augustine's final utterance, in a letter written to Darius, the Roman emperor who made peace with the Vandals without bloodshed or a battle, was: "Those who fight, if they are good men, doubtless seek for peace; nevertheless it is through blood. . . . It is a higher glory to slay war itself with the word than by the sword, and to maintain peace by peace, rather than by war."[18] Here Augustine finally recognized that peace is a means as well as an end but too late. He was old and dying. And it was not his example but that of a Roman emperor which excelled here. Augustine's teachings allowing Christians to engage in warfare affected the whole spectrum of man's political and religious life for centuries to come. He incorporated the Roman policy of the just war into a Christian theology of the just war. He laid down qualifications to be sure, but he opened a breech which only widened through the middle ages. Rather than the theory remaining a qualification, it became a license.

Violence was consecrated by the papacy at the end of the Clarmont Synod in 1095 when Pope Urban launched a dramatic appeal to the entire Christian church to begin a holy war against Islam. He said:

> Most beloved brethren, moved by the exigencies of the times, I, Urban, wearing by permission of God the papal tiara, and spiritual ruler of the whole world, have come to you, the servants of God, as a messenger to disclose the divine admonition. . . . You must carry succor to your brethren dwelling in the East, and needing your aid, which they have so often demanded. For the Turks, a Persian people, have attacked them. . . . Wherefore, I pray and exhort, nay not I, but the Lord prays and exhorts you, as heralds of Christ, by frequent exhortation, to urge men of all ranks, knights and foot soldiers, rich and poor, to hasten to exterminate this vile race from the lands of our brethren, and to bear timely aid to the worshippers of Christ. I speak to those who are present, I proclaim it to the absent, but Christ commands. Moreover, the sins of those who set out thither, if they lose their lives on the journey, by land or sea, or in fighting against the heathen, shall be remitted in that hour; this I grant to all who go, through the power of God vested in me.[19]

Urban's motive was to bring the Western and Eastern church back together by uniting against a common foe, Islam. He used a bad means, war. But did he achieve his end? No. Jerususalem is not in Christian hands today. The Eastern and Western churches are divided and have been since the time of Urban. Violence begets violence and is never ultimately successful. But here we have the pope in Rome codifying Augustine's thoughts into papal commands for war—a "just" war, not of defense but of aggression sanctified by God through his temporal vicar, the pope. The teachings of Augustine made possible Urban's holy war which was not consistent with the teaching of Jesus.

Thomas Aquinas

By the time of the twelfth and thirteenth centuries,

the just war theory became legalized in form through the writings of Gratian and the scholastic firmness of Aquinas in the thirteenth century, whose words today are authoritative among Roman Catholics. In an 1899 encyclical, "Aetorni Patrie," Pope Leo XIII made the philosophy of Aquinas the official philosophy of the Catholic Church.

The most complete statement by Thomas Aquinas on war can be found in the *Summa Theologica*, Part 2, question 40, Of War, "First Article, Whether It Is Always Sinful to Wage War?" Aquinas wrote:

> We proceed thus to the first article: Objection 1. It would seem that it is always sinful to wage war. Because punishment is not inflicted except for sin. Now those who wage war are threatened by our Lord with punishment, according to Matthew 26:52: All that take the sword shall perish with the sword. Therefore all wars are unlawful.
>
> Objection 2. Further, Whatever, is contrary to Divine precept is a sin. But war is contrary to Divine precept, for it is written (Matthew 5:39): But I say to you not to resist evil; and (Romans 12:19): not revenging yourselves, my dearly beloved, but give place unto wrath. Therefore war is always sinful. . . .
>
> I answer that, In order for a war to be just, three things are necessary. First, the authority of the sovereign by whose command the war is to be waged. For it is not the business of the private individual to declare war, because he can seek for redress of his rights from the tribunal of his superior. Moreover, it is not the business of the private individual to summon together the people, what has to be done in wartime. And as the care of the common weal is committed to those who are in authority, it is their business to watch over the common weal of the city, kingdom, or province subject to them. And just as it is lawful for them to have recourse to the sword in defending the common weal against internal disturbances, when they punish evil-doers, according to the words of the apostle (Romans 13:4): He beareth not the sword

in vain; for he is God's minister, an avenger to execute wrath upon him who doeth evil; so too, it is their business to have recourse to the sword of war in defending the common weal against external enemies. Hence it is said of those who are in authority (Psalm 82:4); Rescue the poor; and deliver the needy out of the hand of the sinner; and for this reason Augustine says (Contra Faust., XXII. 75): The natural order conducive to peace among mortals demands that the power to declare and counsel war should be in the hands of those who hold the supreme authority.

Secondly, a just cause is required, namely that those who are attacked, should be attacked because they deserve it on account of some fault. Wherefore Augustine says in Hept., qu.x: A just war is one to be described as one that avenges wrongs, when a nation or state has to be punished, for refusing to make amends for the wrongs inflicted by its subjects, or to restore what it had seized unjustly.

Thirdly, it is necessary that the beligerent should have a rightful intention, so that they intend the advancement of good, or the avoidance of evil. . . . For it may happen that the war is declared by the legitimate authority, and for a just cause, and yet rendered unlawful through a wicked intention. . . ."

Reply Objection 1. As Augustine says (Contra Faust., XXII. 70): To take the sword is to arm oneself in order to take the life of anyone, without the command or permission of superior or lawful authority. On the other hand, to have recourse to the sword (as a private person) by the authority of the sovereign or judge, or (as a public person) through zeal for justice, and by the authority, so to speak, of God, is not to take the sword, but to use it as commissioned by another, wherefore it does not deserve punishment. And yet even those who make sinful use of the sword are not always slain with the sword, yet they always perish with their own sword, because, unless they repent, they are punished eternally for their sinful use of the sword.

Reply Objection 2. Such like precepts . . . should always be borne in readiness of mind, so that we be ready to obey

> them, and if necessary, to refrain from resistance or self-defense. Nevertheless it is necessary sometimes for a man to act otherwise for the common good, or the good of those with whom he is fighting. Hence Augustine says (Letter to Marcellus): Those whom we have to punish with a kindly severity, it is necessary to handle in many ways against their will. For when we are stripping a man of the lawlessness of sin, it is good for him to be vanquished, since nothing is more hopeless than the happiness of sinners, whence arises a guilty impunity, and an evil will, like an internal enemy.[20]

Aquinas codified Augustine's teaching and Urban's revelation, and there was no turning back to the peace of the gospel. It is not surprising that this age is replete with war.

Francis of Assisi

Prior to the Reformation, Francis of Assisi is well known for his personal lifestyle of nonviolence. Francis stands out with non-Catholics as their favorite among the Catholic saints.[21] He lived shortly before Aquinas. His message of peace still speaks to all mankind by his personal practice of Christian nonviolence. But Francis in no way contested the use of violence by the church as a tenet of moral theology.

In the time of Francis, the Roman Catholic Church was *the* Christian Church. After Francis and his followers decided to live a life based on poverty, simplicity, and humility, they went to Rome and asked for the pope's approval of their undertaking. Francis demonstrated his obedience to the pope and to the church and felt that was the way a Christian should live. But Francis also believed that his band of laymen should follow the teachings of Jesus in the Sermon on the Mount and the instructions of Jesus for preaching. Francis instructed his followers not to bear arms, not to take oaths, to be content with one cloak, one pair of sandals, and no other possessions, to carry no weapons, and to go from town to town preaching repentance. And this is what they did. Francis established a First Order for celibate men, a Second Order for celibate women, and a Third Order for married men and women. The life of the first order appeared quite severe to outsiders. The bishop of Assisi summoned Francis to him and said, "It seems to me that your life is going to be very hard and austere if you really set out to have no possessions at all." But Francis was ready for this. "My lord," he said, "if we have possessions we shall need arms to protect them. And from this arises disputes and quarrels and love of God and one's neighbor is much hindered. This is why we do not wish to possess any worldly goods." The bishop could say no more.[22]

The same author writes that about this time "Christendom was greatly troubled. Could she hold her own against forces so great [referring to the threat of the Mongol horde from Asia]? Could another and even greater effort be made to rally the faithful to give their best in the cause of God's holy war and, crushing the heathen, make Europe safe for Christianity forever or was there perhaps another and better way of meeting the great forces — the way not of the sword but of the cross, not a force but of love? Could there be found men who were willing to go unarmed among the heathen hordes and risk torture, persecution, and death in the cause of peace, as their brothers so gallantly risked their lives in war?"[23]

Moorman concludes that St. Francis had shown them the way with his new order of Christianity. But his witness of poverty and nonviolence was difficult for the civilian magistrates to recognize, and slowly but surely the control of Franciscans passed from Francis to the pope with the appointment of a protector for the order. Much of the early witness of Francis was compromised.

Soon Franciscans had the use of many worldly possessions, even though as far as the letter of the law was concerned, they didn't own them. Ownership was held by the papacy for use by the Franciscans. Soon Franciscans did not have to live in poverty, and members of the Third Order could become violent. By this time St. Elzear, a devout and prominent tertiary, led an army into battle and John of Capistrano and James the March became inquisitors with the express purpose of stamping out troublesome congregations. Torture was to be used if necessary to extract information from potential heretics. St. Bernardino implored Christians to have nothing to do with Jews, and said that if he had his way "all Jews would wear special marks on their clothes so that every one would recognize them and avoid them." By 1289 "the Order now was very different from what it had been in its origin, the friar no longer a harmless evangelist and preacher but secure, privileged, well-housed, well-fed, and given every opportunity for learning and study."[24]

St. Francis lived a life of agony in his latter years because of the gradual abandonment of his ideals by his order. He ultimately left his own Order and sought solice as a hermit on a mountainside. Some Franciscans believed that Francis had pointed the way toward the life of Christ and continued to preach about the poverty of Christ. Yet by AD 1323 any Franciscan who continued to preach about the poverty of Christ was liable to arrest. Four Franciscans were burned to death for attempting to follow the original way of St. Francis which in effect was the original way of Jesus. When Francis died much of his spirit of poverty and nonviolence died with him.

The story of Francis is also the story of Christian nonviolence. Should Catholics be content with this ending or should the suffering of Francis, loving and nonresistant to the end, be an inspiration to modern Catholics to make the church right again? God told Francis to repair his church.

Francis misunderstood at first. He thought God meant a church of stones and mortar. But God told Francis he meant a church of the spirit. He is telling this to us too.

Erasmus

Just before the Reformation, Erasmus provided the church with an issue of reform far more important than those the violent Luther and Calvin proposed a few years later. No advocate of revolution or reaction, but a real critic of the violent church, Erasmus said in 1514:

> If one would consider well but the behavior and shape of man's body, shall he not forthwith perceive that nature, or rather God, hath shaped this creature, not to war, but to friendship, not to destruction, but to health, not to wrong, but to kindness and benevolence. For whereas nature hath armed all other beasts with their own armor, as the violence of the bulls, she has armed with horns; the ramping lion with claws; to the boar she hath given the mashing tusks; she hath armed the elephant with a long trunk-snout, besides his great huge body and hardness of skin . . . some she provideth to save by swiftness of flight, as doves; and to some she hath given venom instead of a weapon; to some she hath given a much horrible and ugly look . . . man alone she hath brought forth all naked, weak, tender, and without any armor, with most soft flesh and smooth skin. There is nothing at all in all these members that may seem to be ordained to war, or to any violence."[25]

Although Erasmus seemed to advocate war under certain circumstances when he said, "A good prince should never go to war at all unless, after trying every other means, he cannot possibly avoid it," he questioned whether there was any excuse for going to war at all. He concluded that "the pontifical laws do not disapprove of war. Augustine approves of it in some instances and St. Bernard praises some soldiers. But Christ Himself and Peter and Paul everywhere teach the opposite. Why is their authority less with us than that of Augustine and Bernard?"[26]

In his *Praise of Folly*, Erasmus analyzed the justification for violence by those who act upon Jesus' advice to His disciples to sell their cloaks and buy a sword. Why did Jesus ask His disciples to do this? If He had not instructed them to buy a sword, Jesus would not have been in the position to demonstrate upon His arrest that they should refrain from violence by the use of a sword, and that He was not a political revolutionary or military Messiah. Until this time they possessed no sword. Obviously Jesus told His apostles to buy swords to demonstrate that he who lives by the sword dies by the sword. Erasmus pointed out the folly of people who use this passage as an example justifying swords. They misunderstand the full message of the gospel.

Truly the accommodation of war by Augustine, Aquinas, and the church is pure folly. *There is no just war.* We need only quote the logic of the German militarist von Clauswitz to understand that war can never be moderated. He says that to "introduce into a philosophy of war a principle of moderation would be an absurdity. War is an act of violence pushed to its utmost bounds."[27]

Luther and Calvin

The Reformation was fought on other matters more detailed, procedural, legalistic, and less spiritual than the question of war and peace. Violence and nonviolence apparently were not issues in the dispute between the pope and Luther. Both Luther and Calvin advocated violence as did Aquinas and the pope. Each justified capital punishment and wars. Luther asked, "What is the form of love applicable in a particular situation — to endure justice or demand justice?"[28] "Enduring justice" was to suffer evil "without avenging oneself."[29] Luther relied heavily on Augustine;

both saw violence as a means toward love, killing as a means toward peace. Luther chose to demand justice.

Luther said, "Therefore, the wrath and severity of the sword is just as necessary to a people as eating and drinking, even life itself."[30] This is not the place to expound on Luther's two-kingdoms doctrine, but this theory explains his views on the relation of the spiritual and secular world for Christians. The government, according to Luther, was God ordained to prevent chaos and to promote law and order. The Christian may take up the sword for the government and the just war even though he may not do the same for the church. In this respect he differed from the Catholicism of his time which believed that both the church and the state could use the weapon of violence justly against their enemies. Luther believed that in taking up the sword the Christian may maim or kill but should not commit any other sin such as rape, in the process of doing so.[31] He concluded that "the secular sword must be red and bloody for the world will and must be evil."[32]

His theories led him to disown some violence, particularly the violence of insurrection: "No insurrection is ever right no matter what the cause."[33] He admonished Christians to do no violence against the state but only for the state. Later he justified Christian political revolution against the pope in order to preserve the gospel. He also supported the use of violence for the protection of self and neighbor. Here he differed with Augustine who would not justify the use of violence by an individual to protect himself. But for the most part, Lutheranism perpetuated the violence which had dominated the Roman Catholic Church.

Another major branch of Protestantism, Calvinism, was in essential agreement with the Lutherans and Catholics on this point. Calvin advised Christians, "Without any breach of friendship toward their enemies, they may avail themselves of the assistance of the magistrate for the preservation of their property, or, from zeal for the public good, may bring a pestilent offender to justice, though they know he can only be punished with death.[34] Calvin wrote:

> Now, as it is sometimes necessary for kings and nations to take up arms for the infliction of such public vengeance, the same reason will lead us to infer the lawfulness of wars which are undertaken for this end. For if they have been entrusted with power to preserve the tranquility of their own territories, to suppress the seditious tumults of disturbers, to succor the victims of oppression, and to punish crimes — can they exert this power for a better purpose than to repel the violence of him who disturbs both the private repose of individuals and the general tranquility of the nation, who excites insurrections and perpetrates acts of oppression, cruelty, and every species of crime? If they ought to be the guardians and defenders of the laws, it is incumbent upon them to defeat the efforts of all by whose injustice the discipline of the laws is corrupted. And if they justly punish those robbers whose injuries have only extended to a few persons, shall they suffer a whole district to be plundered and devastated with impunity? For there is no difference whether he who in a hostile manner invades, disturbs, and plunders the territory of another to which he has no right be he a king or one of the meanest of mankind: all persons of this description are equally to be considered as robbers, and ought to be punished as such. It is the dictate both of natural equity and of the nature of the office, therefore, that princes are armed, not only to restrain the crimes of private individuals by judicial punishments, but also to defend the territories committed to their charge by going to war against any hostile aggression; and the Holy Spirit, in many passages of Scripture, declares such wars to be lawful.
>
> If it be objected that the New Testament contains no precept or example which proves war to be lawful to Christians, I answer, first, that the reason for waging war which existed in ancient times is equally valid in the present age; and that, on the contrary, there is no cause to prevent

> princes from defending their subjects. Secondly, that no express declaration on this subject is the be expected in the writings of the apostles, whose design was not to organize civil governments, but to describe the spiritual kingdom of Christ. Lastly that in those very writings it is implied, by the way, that no change has been made in this respect by the coming of Christ. "For," to use the words of Augustine, "if Christian discipline condemned all war, the soldiers who inquired respecting their salvation ought rather to have been directed to cast away their arms, and entirely to renounce the military profession; whereas the advice given them was, 'Do violence to no man, neither accuse any falsely; and be content with your wages.' An injunction to be content with their wages was certainly not a prohibition of the military life."[35]

Augustine's reasoning concerning John the Baptist's statement would lead us to believe that because Jesus did not specifically condemn slavery, He approved of it.

Calvin chose to use Augustine for his authority as did Luther. So we can trace the justified violence theory in Protestantism back through Calvinism and Lutheranism to Augustine. Interestingly, Augustine's quote used by Calvin about violence refers to the words of John the Baptist prior to his meeting with Jesus and also prior to Jesus' statement on the Sermon on the Mount.

During the Reformation, however, there was a divergence from the Protestantism of Luther in the form of the Anabaptists, and eventual development of small Protestant sects, now called the peace churches, such as the Brethren, Mennonites, and the Quakers, who preserved the message of the Sermon on the Mount in respect to war. Quaker George Fox, Mennonite Menno Simons, and Brethren Alexander Mack taught that Christians should follow Jesus' example. If ever we are to resolve the question of violence, it will only be done by looking to Jesus and His way today, the way of peace and love.

Part III

Quo Vadis:
Jesus or Caesar?

CHAPTER 7

Encyclical, Council, and Synod

The justified violence tradition remained essentially unchanged in Christendom during the five centuries following the Reformation. Modern Catholic teaching does not vary from the pronouncements of Augustine and Aquinas. In a Catholic treatise on social ethics written in the 1950s, Messner said:

> St. Thomas, in fact, leaves no doubt on the matter, and he frequently appeals to the authority of St. Augustine. The discussion of the virtues of patience and fortitude, and of the virtues in war, gives him occasion to discover the divergence between the findings of political ethics and of individual ethics. He is occupied with the question of how far the state itself is bound by the precepts of Christ, and the apostles, expressed in the Sermon on the Mount, and elsewhere, such

as: "But I say to you not to resist the evil: but if one strike thee on the right cheek, turn to him also the other" (Matthew 5:39). Or, "Revenge not yourselves . . . but give place unto wrath, for it is written: Revenge is mine. I will repay, sayeth the Lord" (Romans 12:19). With Augustine he replies: "These precepts constitute a universal obligation of spiritual preparedness to accept injustice with patience, and not to defend oneself, but they do not demand the same type of action in every case."[1]

Messner goes on to say:

One of the gravest dilemmas of conscience into which reason of state can plunge a statesman is the decision for or against war, and the means of national defense. We are thinking of course, solely of a just, defensive war. . . . Absolute pacifism denies any justification to purely defensive war. We need not repeat the arguments by which natural law philosophy today as ever holds that under certain conditions defensive war is justified. It is no real objection to these arguments to say that non-violent, purely passive resistance is a method more likely to succeed in the defense of a nation's highest good, such as its moral and religious existence. For there is ample evidence in recent history that the modern totalitarian, aggressor state may well be able to destroy the spiritual individuality of a nation. Besides that, there can be no doubt that a nation engaged in a war of defense, conscious that its spiritual and moral existence is the issue, can summon up moral forces which even in the event of external defeat can be of untold importance for the continuance of the struggle by the then solely remaining means of passive resistance. When absolute pacifism appears to the Christian conscience in support of the opposition, to defensive war, it presumes to anticipate Providence, by determining not withstanding circumstances, the manner of trial which a people will receive from the hand of the Ruler of history. The pacifist decides independently for non-violent, passive resistance. Yet how can he say whether active, armed resistance by a state as prescribed by moral reason of state, may not, even if not actually condemned to failure, decide moral and spiritual

> existence and so the whole future of a nation? We have already heard from no less an authority than St. Thomas that this is not always the sense in which are to be understood the word of the Apostle that evil is not to be resisted and vengeance must be left to the Lord. It is, rather, the moral function of the state to realize the common good in given circumstances, so far as it lies with human power. Beyond this, to give the moral order its eternal reality, lies in the hand of the Creator.[2]

Messner reemphasized the age-old proposition of Aquinas and Augustine and interpreted the Sermon on the Mount through Aquinas, thus justifying once again the just-war theory. That was also the state of affairs in the sixties. Few studies on the weaknesses of the just-war theory were available at that time.[3] We knew much more of statements such as that of Pius XII that a Catholic was duty bound to help his country in a just war,[4] than Cardinal Ottaviani's statement that modern war was incompatible with a just war.[5]

Probably one of the most popular books in Roman Catholicism, in the first half of the twentieth century, was the *Question Box* first published in 1903. By 1930 it had a circulation of over two million copies. In his preface to the second edition, the then archbishop of New York stated, "May God's blessing continue on the mission of the *Question Box*. May it bring the light of truth to the mind of Catholic and non-Catholic reader. May it move the seeker after truth to pray with the Psalmist, 'Direct me in Thy Truth, and teach me!'"[6]

The *Question Box* expounded on the morality of war as follows: "While recognizing that war is one of the greatest evils that can confront a nation, the Catholic Church has always held that just war is licit and moral. She condemns the pacifism of the Quaker who declares all wars incompatible with Christianity, as well as the pagan view that modern aggressive wars are a nation's right and duty."[7] In scriptural support for this position the *Question Box* cited eight quotations from the Old Testament, John the Baptist's advice to soldiers of his day in Luke 3:14, and the praise of the Centurion in Matthew 8:10. It gave one quotation from the words of Christ (Matthew 5:39) and dismissed it by saying, "Christ's words on the Sermon on the Mount are a counsel of perfection addressed to the individual."[8] The *Question Box* stated that the early fathers did not condemn war as intrinsically immoral, and that any objection to serving in the armies had to do with the danger of apostasy and idolatry and not killing.[9]

American Catholic textbooks used in high schools prior to the Second Vatican Council followed the same line. The benefits of Constantine were lauded: full freedom for Christians, no pagan temples in Constantium, endowment of buildings and land to the church, bishops made judges, churches tax exempt, Sunday a day of rest, money grants for charities, and discouragement of paganism.[10] Not too long after Constantine the pagan title of Pontifix Maximus, which had been held exclusively by the Roman emperors, was transferred to the Roman popes. There is no mention in this textbook that as the result of obtaining these material gifts the Christian church began to justify the violence of the Roman empire as the new way for Christendom.

A modern Catholic American history textbook states that "such conquistadores as Cortez and Pizarro braved the resistance of the ancient stronghold."[11] No wonder we as Christians have been prone to war and hostile to Indians when textbooks were written creating these impressions. Even that liberal bastion of the Catholic Church, the Paulists, published a book in 1973 entiteld *Peace, War and the Young Catholic* which states: "It seems clear that a war of aggression cannot be justified under any circumstances while a war of defense against unjust aggression may be justified."[12]

The natural law philosophers of Catholicism, and their successors in Protestantism, seem not far from the anti-pacifistic viewpoints of Stalin, Mao Tse-tung, and Hitler. Hitler wrote in *Mein Kampf:*

> Thus, the pacifist, by giving himself subjectively and entirely to his idea, will, in the presence of any menace to his people, be it ever so grave and unjust, always (insofar as he is a German) seek after the objective right and never from pure instinct of self-preservation join the ranks of his herd and fight with them. . . . Our German pacifist will accept in silence the bloodiest rape of our nation at the hands of the most vicious military powers if the change in this state of affairs can be achieved only by resistance — that is, force — for this would be contrary to the spirit of his peace society.[13]

Hitler considered the pacifist as a thorn in his side. He said:

> Anyone, for example, who really desired the victory of the pacifistic idea in this world with all his heart would have to fight with all the means at his disposal for the conquest of the world by the Germans; for, if the opposite should occur the last pacifist would die out with the last German, since the rest of the world has never fallen so deeply as our own people, unfortunately, has for this nonsense so contrary to Nature and reason. Then, if we were serious, whether we like it or not, we would have to wage wars in order to arrive at pacifism.[14]

This is nothing more than saying we have to fight wars in order to gain peace, a view very much like Augustine's. Hitler also said that a pacifist should not make his own subjective determination on whether to fight or not. This sounds a lot like Messner. And, of course, like Christian exponents of violence, Hitler called on God for His support: "Hence today I believe that I am acting in accordance with the will of the Almighty Creator; by defending myself against the Jew, I am fighting for the work of the Lord."[15]

The first glimmer of a new spirit in the Catholic tradition came with Pope John. His statements in *Pacem in Terris* put forth a new perspective on war and peace. John XXIII said, "There can be or at least there should be no doubt that relations between states as between individuals, should be regulated not by the force of arms but by the light of reason, by the rule, that is, of truth, of justice, and of active and sincere cooperation."[16] He quoted Pius XII: "Violence has always achieved only destruction."[17] Pope John declared that peace is to be found not in "equality of arms but in mutual trust alone."[18] Finally he said: "And God will never fail to act on his interior being, with the result that a person, who at a given moment of his life who lacked clarity of faith or even adheres to erroneous doctrines, can at a future date be enlightened and believe in the truth."[19]

The recent statements of the Council in Vatican II told us that "Divine Providence urgently demands that we free ourselves from the age-old slavery of war"[20] and that "we cannot fail to praise those who renounce the use of violence in the vindication of their rights."[21] However, according to Richard McSorley, author of *Kill for Peace?* the Council fathers were unable entirely to share John's vision, but his vision was put before them and they responded in some measure.[22] Pope John cautioned us that "in an age such as ours, which prides itself on its atomic energy, it is contrary to reason to believe that war is now a suitable way to restore rights which have been violated."[23] John did not say that offensive war or defensive war is contrary to reason. He said that all war is contrary to reason.[24]

Pope John seems to have more faith than did the clerics of Vatican II when he reminded us that God will never fail to act on our interior being. Therefore it is not necessary for man to act on another individual's exterior being by violence! He commanded us to mutual trust alone. John said further, "The fundamental principal on which our present peace depends must be replaced by another which declares that the true and solid peace of nations consist not on the quality of arms but on mutual trust alone. We believe that this can be brought to pass, and we consider that it is something which reason requires, that it is eminently desirable in itself, and that it will prove to be the source of many benefits."[25]

Vatican II

A careful comparison of *Pacem in Terris* and Vatican II reveals that Vatican II is not a carbon copy of *Pacem in Terris.*[26] The Vatican Council focused on nuclear war and stated that "any act of war aimed indiscriminately at the destruction of entire cities or extensive areas along with their population is a crime against God and man himself. It merits unequivocable and unhesitating condemnation." But where are those who will say that the indiscriminate destruction of entire cities and extensive areas, even by the allies in World War II or in Korea or in Vietnam and Cyprus is a crime against God and man himself? There does not seem to be any war, large or small, that does not engage in indiscriminant destruction of entire cities or extensive areas. To begin with — how do we define a city? How many people in the city must be killed? How much destruction of extensive areas must be accomplished for it to be a crime against God and man himself? But although Vatican II asked us to undertake an evaluation of war with an entirely new attitude, it "refuses to call for total renouncement of force by individual nations until an adequate security force actually exists."[27]

It continues: "As long as the danger of war remains and there is no competent and sufficiently powerful authority at the international level, governments cannot be denied the right to legitimate defense when every means of peaceful settlement has been exhausted."[28] Vatican II leaves us with the instruction not to destroy cities on the one hand. It seems to abolish the aggressive "just" war, such as the Crusades, but to continue the defensive "just" war even in a nuclear age.

The position of Vatican II on just war fell short of Pope John's pronouncement in *Pacem in Terris,* and continued to recognize retaliation as Christian, and multilateral approaches as more acceptable than unilateral solutions. We must ask whether the turning of the other cheek is multilateral or unilateral and whether the instruction not to resist the evildoer is an instruction against any retaliation? Unfortunately Vatican II did not reach the moral imperative of the Sermon on the Mount. Some prelates emerged at least as nuclear pacifists. Cardinal Alfrink took the position that a just war is no longer possible holding that "the existence of nuclear weapons excludes the existence of a just war because the means that could be used to fight injustice would cause much greater injustice."[20] Cardinal Lercaro of Bologna dismissed the idea of a just war as something "left over from the cases and mental attitudes which no longer have anything to do with the facts."[30] But it seems that the Council believed that there are certain wars which are moral for Christians to wage.

Because the Sermon on the Mount holds that all violence is immoral, and therefore all war, much work remains to be done for the church in its return to the original meaning of the gospels. This work should then be the immediate task of Christians so that the Council's hope, expressed in the words of Isaiah 2:4 will become a reality: "They shall beat their swords into plowshares, and their spears into pruning hooks; one nation shall not raise sword against another, nor shall they train for war again."[31]

A Council which said, "Those who are pledged to the service of their country as members of the armed forces should regard themselves as the agents of security and freedom on behalf of their people," and a Council which stated, "As long as they fulfill this role properly, they are making a genuine contribution to the establishment of peace,"[32] could not have reached back to the commands of the Sermon on the Mount. The Council remains awkwardly straddled between war and peace in saying that it is possible to love in war. The Council continues the admonitions of Aquinas and Augustine to make war in moderation, but the experts on war tell us that to make war successfully, compromise and moderation may never be considered. Jesus tells us to make peace — and this also must be done without compromise.

In 1971 and 1972 the Synod of Roman Catholic Bishops met in Rome, and it was hoped that the great issues of justice and peace would be reexamined by a Pontifical Commission and the Synod in the light of the Christian witness reminiscent of the early church.

The Apostolic Letter

Pope Paul's apostolic letter of May 14, 1971, indicated:

> From all sides there rises a yearning for more justice and a desire for a better guaranteed peace in mutual respect among individuals and peoples.[33] . . . Some of her members are tempted by radical and violent solutions from which

> they believe they can expect a happier outcome. While some people, unaware of present injustices, strive to prolong the existing situation, others allow themselves to be beguiled by revolutionary ideologies which promise them, not without delusion, a definitely better world. . . . It is up to the Christian communities to analyze with objectivity the situation which is proper to their own country, to shed on it the light of the Gospels' unalterable words and to draw up principles of reflections, norms of judgment and directives for action from the social teaching of the Church. . . . Christians must first of all renew their confidence in a forcefulness and special character of the demands made by the Gospel. The Gospel is not out-of-date because it was proclaimed, written and lived in a different socio-cultural context.[34] . . . Love for man, the prime value of the earthly order, insures the conditions for peace, both social peace and international peace, by affirming our universal brotherhood.[35]

Pertaining to ideologies and human liberties, the pope told us that man

> cannot adhere to the Marxist ideology, to its dialectic of violence and to the way it absorbs individual freedom in the collectivity, at the same time denying all transcendence to man and his personal and collective history; nor can he adhere to the liberal ideology which believes it exalts individual freedom by withdrawing it from every limitation, by stimulating it through exclusive seeking of interest and power, and by considering social solidarities as more or less automatic consequences of individual initiatives, not as an aim and a major criterion of the value of the social organization. . . . The Christian faith is above and is sometimes opposed to the ideologies, in that it recognizes God, who is transcendent and the Creator, and who, through all the levels of creation, calls on man as endowed with responsibility and freedom.[36]

With further reference to totalitarian and coercive characteristics of ideologies, the pope said: "And people imagine they find in it a justification for their activity, even violent activity, and an adequate response to a generous desire to serve."[37] He alluded to a possible retreat of ideologies: "It has been possible today to speak of a retreat of ideologies. In this respect the present time may be favorable for an openness to the concrete transcendence of Christianity."[38]

In one of his few sentences related to peace, Paul stated, "Animated by the power of the Spirit of Jesus Christ, the Savior of mankind, and upheld by hope, the Christian involves himself in the building up of a human city, one that is to be peaceful, just, and fraternal and acceptable as an offering to God."[39]

> There is a need to establish a greater justice in the sharing of goods, both within national communities and on the international level. In international exchanges there is a need to go beyond relationships based on force, in order to arrive at agreements reached with the good of all in mind. Relationships based on force have never in fact established justice in a true and lasting manner, even if at certain times the alternation of position can often make it possible to find easier conditions for dialogue. The use of force moreover leads to the setting in motion of opposing forces, and from this springs a climate of struggle which opens a way to situations of extreme violence and to abuses. . . . Thus it is necessary to have the courage to undertake a revision of the relationships between nations.[40] . . . The Church invites all Christians to take up a double task of inspiring and of innovating, in order to make structures evolve, so as to adapt them to the real needs of today.[41]

Justice in the World

The Pontifical Commission's document, "*Justice in the World, An Exposition of Topics to Be Discussed in the Second General Session,*" which was considered in Rome in 1971. opened by stating: "New historical situations . . . demand an honest reexamination of the Christian message, a courageous return to the heart of the gospel. Only in this way will the Word of Christ become a word of truth and of life for the present-day world."[42]

In paragraph 18, it discussed the effects of war and peace upon us:

> There is the fact of swollen budgets for war and defense. Some nations adduce these budgets as a principal reason for their paltry contribution to aid. Such a situation certainly cannot fail to disturb men's consciences; astronomical sums spent for war (or in anticipation of the eventual possibility of war) and a derisory sum contributed to the war against world poverty. The fact of an arms race, mobilizing today's devastating potentialities of destruction, must be considered an injustice to the millions of potential victims and to the hundreds of millions of people compelled to live under the constant dread of a third world war with the devastation it would unleash.[43]

These words echo Patriarch Maximus when in 1964 he said to the Council:

> "For the love of Christ, Who is Friend of Men and King of Peace, we earnestly supplicate you to pronounce a solemn and forceful condemnation of all nuclear, chemical, and bacteriological war. Let this sacred Council address a message to the world on the model of the one prepared at the outset of the Council's proceedings, condemning, in principle, all nuclear war, under all its forms, and demanding that the millions saved on disarmament be devoted to the alleviation of human poverty in a world where two thirds of the population does not have enough to eat and is in dire need."[44]

The Catholic bishops, long devoted to justice, were long overdue in their devotion to peace.

The document continued, under the heading, "The Church Questions Itself":

> It is clear that the lay apostolate and the Church's social action as well as those other movements of Christian inspiration active in the temporal order, and there are many, have helped effect an ever growing Christian presence in the world. In all this effort of local Churches and of Christians, it is not surprising that hesitations, confusion, and even conflict arise among Christians themselves. To some, their brothers seem no longer interested in the sacred and eternal, but rather to be caught up exclusively in temporal concerns, and that sometimes even at the price of accepting conflict and violence. . . . All these efforts, these hesitations, these attempts at solution, guided all by a virtually identical understanding of the Church's universal mission, must be critically evaluated if the Church is to be completely at the service of man."[45]

And further, "For her part the Church may have no worldly ambition unworthy of her mission, but must aim instead at one goal; to continue the work of Christ who came into the world to bear witness to the truth, who came to save and not to condemn, to serve and not be served."[46] The document thereupon attempted to relate justice and Christian love and cited "the First Epistle of St. John which states emphatically that only he who loves his neighbor truly, in deeds, knows and loves God and is really just. (See 1 John 3:10-23; and 4:8, 19-21.) Being a true disciple of Christ means not only believing in the truth, in Christ (John 14:6), but also, and to no lesser degree acting in the truth (John 3:20, 21), in love, and in service of one's neighbor (John 15:10 17 and 13:34).[47] . . . Thc carly Christians followed Christ's teachings by sharing their material goods with other members of their community(Acts 2:44, 45) and sharing them in mutual help among different communities (2 Corinthians 8:1-24) and in life of brotherly equality amongst all (James 2:1-13). . . . Charity is above all a demand for justice, that is to say, the concrete recognition of every man's rights on an individual as well as collective level."[48]

In its concluding paragraphs, the document said:

> We have arrived at a critical moment of human history, one that demands that the Church give full force to her message. The present-day situation appears as a real challenge to Christianity. The Church must appear as responsible for Christ's message to the world. . . . The Church may make all the efforts in the world in defense of the truth of her message; but if she does not authenticate it by love shown in action, this Christian message risks losing the sight of credibility for men of today. The Church launches her appeal to all Christians as such that as Christians they take up man's defense in the name of the Gospel and of Christian love."[49]

But after reaching that crescendo, the report fell back upon traditional political viewpoints, echoed the negative parts of Vatican II, the old theories of Aquinas and Augustine, and the political temporality of Constantine the Great:

> It might be well here to bring to the attention of youth, that in certain situations in which fundamental rights of the person are seriously threatened, recourse to force in support of these rights may be lawful, provided that all legal means have been explored. But at the same time, it should never be forgotten that force is suited to demolishing rather than to building up. The construction of a more just world calls for competence, adequate means, a spirit of initiative, understanding, agreement; construction that can be realized only gradually by laying one stone upon another.[50]

Why this admonition to the "youth"? The youth have threatened violence, and they have used violence. But some of the older members of society have used it before, and others have copied them. Even some Catholic priests use violent means, justifying their actions because "all other means have been explored." Could not each one of us at any given time justify the use of violence on the very same basis? Were not the Crusades couched in just such terminology? Were not the Inquisitions derived from such beliefs? If we are to justify violence on that score, then who are we to judge a particular age-group in this world from copying us in using violence as a just means to a good end? Rather we should teach that when we refuse to follow Jesus, we may not say that all other means have been explored.

For this reason it is imperative now that old and young alike must be made aware of the Maximilians of the past. Violence begets violence as Tolstoy said, and if we justify the use of violence in this way for ourselves, we justify the use of violence for others according to their interpretation of what justifies its ultimate use.

The document, *Justice in the World*, calls on us to reexamine the Christian message for a courageous return to the heart of the gospel, and tell us further that if we proceed along this line we will succeed, because in the words of Isaiah, "I have endowed him with my spirit that he may bring true justice to the nations. . . . He will neither waver, nor be crushed until true justice is established on earth."[51] Isaiah foretold that the Messiah would be with us until justice is established on earth. So let us proceed, acting upon the demand of the Pontifical Commission, to make an honest reexamination of the Christian message in hope of a courageous return to the heart of the gospel.

In doing so we may reflect upon the Commission's statement which reminds us of the early Christian lifestyle of community living and sharing of goods. We would simply add that it was not only their sharing, but the characteristic of pacifism which also exemplified the lifestyle of the early Christians. Unfortunately the document makes no mention of the early Christian avoidance of violence and war. An honest reexamination of the Christian message and a courageous return to the heart of the gospel must include a restudy of the lifestyle of pacifism exemplified by the Messiah and His followers until the time of Constantine.

In embarking on this return to the Scriptures, and to the lifestyle emerging from those words, we pray to be "animated by the power of the Spirit of Jesus Christ, the Savior of mankind, and upheld by hope," as Pope Paul stated in his letter[52] so that we as Christians may involve ourselves in the building up of the human city — one that is to be peaceful, just, and fraternal and acceptable as an offering to God. Pope Paul tells us that "love for man, the prime value of the earthly order, ensures the conditions for peace, both social peace and international peace, by affirming our universal brotherhood."[53] Where is this love for people that insures the conditions for peace?

The apostolic letter and the Pontifical Commission report laid the groundwork for the Bishops' Synods of 1971 and 1972. But nothing fundamentally new on pacifism and nonviolence has emerged since with the possible exception of a new attitude towards personal conscientious objection. Pope John's encyclical remains the closest approach to Catholic reconciliation with its early Christian counterparts.

Perhaps the resistance of the Catholic Church to this change in part caused Catholic priests such as Daniel and Philip Berrigan to question that leadership, as well as the leadership of their country, and to offer an alternative to both. Is the pacifism of the Berrigans an alternative which would restore to Catholics the Christian nonviolence of Jesus?

CHAPTER 8

The Confusion of Christians

Modern Catholics and Christian Peace

The failure of the Roman Catholic Church to abolish the war ethic, and to return to the true nature of Christian peace as taught by Christ, weighed heavily on the events surrounding the anti-Vietnam war movements of the late sixties and early seventies. Many Catholics were caught in a conflict of values, arising out of the war, between a duty of justice to aid a defenseless nation, and a duty to God not to kill.

Traditional Catholics had been encouraged to look not to the Scriptures, or to the lives of the early Christians for guidance, but rather to the authoritative pronouncements of their priests, who in turn looked to their bishops, who in turn looked to the pope. And Pope Paul had spoken through the Second Vatican Council and the Synods in favor of the continuation of the just war. So, many Catholics resolved their anxieties by relying on the authority of the church.

For some Catholics, however, this basic contradiction in loving and killing one's enemy caused them to look elsewhere for answers.[1] Two Catholic priests, Daniel and Philip Berrigan rose to the front of the antiwar movement in the late sixties and represented a new Catholic element in the movement for the first time. There had been others before, but none so activist and none so publicized by the press as these.

Many youth had been saying all along that it was about time that the church involved itself in the efforts for peace. The Berrigans did, and they became associated with an unorthodox Catholic stance on peace at a time when the Catholic Church was unwilling to accept the responsibility. But is the Berrigan approach to peace the sort of nonviolence of which Jesus preached? Or is Berriganism just another variation of the just war theory supporting violence by Catholics in the name of peace, and therefore more Augustinian in nature than one might be led to suppose? Is it different only in that in this case it is wrong for the government but right for the oppressed to use it?

In an early Seventies article in *The Ecumenist*, described as "A Journal for Promoting Christian Unity," a letter from Daniel Berrigan to the Weathermen was published with this preamble: "The following letter condensed from a tape addressed by Daniel Berrigan to the Weathermen underground is an interesting Christian statement of conscience, combining a radical rejection of contemporary culture and its institutions with a moving plea for compassion and nonviolence."[2]

Berrigan stated in this letter: "I'm trying to say when people look about them for lives to run with and when hopeless people look for hope, the gift we can offer others is so simple a thing as hope. As they said about Che, as they say about Jesus, some people, even to this day, he gave us hope. So that my hope is that you see your lives in somewhat this way which is to say I hope your lives are about something more than sabotage. I'm certain they are. I hope the sabotage question is tactical and peripheral."[3]

Berrigan continued, "A sensible humane movement operates on several levels at once if it is to get anywhere. So it is saying communication, yes, organizing, yes, community, yes, sabotage, yes — as a tool. This is a conviction that took us where we went. And it took us beyond, to this night. We reasoned that the effect of our act could not be to impede the war or much less to stop the war in its tracks. God help us, if that had been our intentions, we were certainly fools before the fact and doubly fools after it, for in fact the war went on. And still we undertook sabotage long before any of you."[4]

Contrast the words of Berrigan with the words of Gandhi who said, "Sabotage is a form of violence."[5] Berrigan advocated property violence and sabotage as a Christian priest, but nevertheless he said:

> We do violence unwillingly, bar exception as instruments, knowing that the destruction of property is only a means in keeping the end as vivid and urgent and as alive to us as are the means so that the means are judged in every instance by their relation to the ends. I have a great fear of American violence, not only out there in the military and diplomacy, in economics, in industry and advertising, but also in here, in me, up close, among us. On the other hand, I must say, I have very little fear, from firsthand experience, of the violence of the Vietcong or Panthers (I hesitate to use the word violence), for their acts come from the proximate threat of extinction, from being invariably put on the line

> of self-defense, but that's not true of us in our history. . . . Do not ask me why I broke the law, go ask Nixon why he breaks the law constantly, ask the Justice Department, ask the racists. Obviously, but for Johnson and Nixon in their fetching ways, Catonsville would never have taken place and you and I would not be here today, just as but for the same people SDS would never have grown into the Weathermen or the Weathermen have gone underground . . . thank you and shalom.[6]

This in a capsule is Berrigan nonviolence. Apparently neither he nor the Weathermen nor the SDS consider themselves responsible for their violence and therefore, once again, violence is justified to end violence. The Berrigans represent the American peace movement to many Catholics across the world, and to many good people they are the latest apostles of nonviolence.

About the same time a publication, "The Burden of the Berrigans," released by those in support of the brothers, contained only one article criticizing them all. That article was heavily criticized in the publication itself by other authors who apparently had a copy of the critical article before it went to press. Father Greeley, a Chicago priest, wrote in that article that "even if Father Berrigan pauses just short of advocating violence, his position necessarily will lead to violence because it is a position which preaches hatred for American society and hatred for 90 percent of the people who are so immoral as to accept the society's legitimacy and disapprove of his 'liturgical gestures.'[7] Greeley was heavily criticized, but the Berrigans were described as "powerful witnesses," "legitimate prophets," "men for new horizons," and were compared to Amos, Isaiah, Jeremiah, and Ezekiel.

The Jews waited for a political Messiah to revolutionize the government, but they got a pacifist instead who ignored the government and chastised the religionists: a pacifist who refused to use political action to free the slaves, who paid His temple taxes, who told us to lay down our swords, who was available for arrest, who was tortured, and who died bravely. But since Constantine, the Catholic Church has caused laymen and clergy to look to political action as the best means for the resolution of their concerns. One pope divided the political world between Spain and Portugal in the Western Hemisphere. Another started the Crusades.

And today, the Roman Catholic Church tries to revolutionize itself. But is it a revolution to replace a conservative priest with a leftist priest when the result is just one more political messiah who destroys the material while preaching the spiritual? Where is the priest who forsakes politics and government once and for all, forsakes the headlines, abstains from political adoration, and takes on the yoke of practicing the revolution of Jesus? The burden is ours: not one more political messiah or two when we need something new — far more revolutionary than political, when we need a revolution of the spirit, another St. Francis, another Maximilian.

No burden this would be but where is he?
Perhaps he is yet to be.
Perhaps not Phil or Daniel B.
Must it be you and me?
Praise the Lord!
He has already come.
His name is Jesus C.

A Catholic peace advocate more in tune with the early Christians but outpublicized by the Berrigans, Dorothy Day wrote in the magazine of the Fellowship of Reconciliation:

In general the *Catholic Worker* takes the position of the

War Resisters, Quakers, and Fellowship of Reconciliation peace groups in not taking part in these actions, the Berrigan destruction of property, on the principal that although it was only property which suffered destruction, we ourselves have suffered violence, vandalism by hostile right wing groups, the beating of individuals, the spoiling of mailing lists and records, the burning of houses and bars,etc. So we repeat the golden rule, "Do unto others what you would have them do unto you,' and its contrary, 'Do not do unto others what you would not have them do unto you.' "[8]

Perhaps if long ago the Catholic Church had held up Dorothy Day as a Christian witness, we would not be faced with the burden of the Berrigans today. Thomas Merton, in an article for *Ave Maria*, commented on the philosophy of the Berrigans as follows: "It may do more than anything else to promote an irresponsible and meaningless use of force in a pseudo-revolution that will only consolidate the power of the police state. Never was it more necessary to understand the importance of genuine non-violence as a power for real change because it is aimed not so much at revolution as at conversion."[9] Merton saw Berrigan violence as "violent to the extent that it meant pushing some good ladies around and destroying some government property."[10]

All this is not to say that the Berrigans are singularly violent. We are all violent when we refuse to practice nonviolence in the manner Jesus taught.

This does not mean, however, that we should refrain from commenting on that part of the Catholic peace movement, as exemplified by the Berrigans, if it seems to be going down the wrong path and needs instruction as to the nature of nonviolence from a Christian perspective. Such instruction is now lacking in the church, and it is for this reason that Berriganism provides a focus for evaluating the Catholic peace movement of today. If we are satisfied with the tenor of the movement then we should do nothing. But if there is something more to Christian peace than what Berriganism embraces today, we should apply it.

The Catholic Church already has had its share of violence justified by its political right wing. It doesn't need further violence from the left. Thomas Aquinas wrote the following in his *Summa Theologica* on the Toleration of Heretics in the thirteenth century:

> I reply that, with regard to heretics, two considerations are to be kept in mind: (1) on their side, (2) on the side of the church. (1) There is the sin, whereby they deserve not only to be separated from the church by excommunication, but also to be shut off from the world by death. For it is a much more serious matter to corrupt faith, through which comes the soul's life, than to forge money, through which temporal life is supported. Hence if forgers of money or other malefactors are straightway put to death by secular princes, with much more justice can heretics, immediately upon conviction be not only excommunicated but also put to death.
>
> (2) But on the side of the Church there is mercy, with the view to the conversion of them that are in error; and therefore the Church does not straightway condemn, but after a first and a second admonition, as the Apostle teaches (Tit. iii, 10). After that, if he be found still stubborn, the Church gives up hope of his conversion and takes thought for the safety of others, by separating him from the Church by sentence of excommunication; and, further leaves him to the secular court, to be exterminated from the world by death. . . .[11]

Little wonder that Catholics like the Berrigans resort to sabotage when they have the example of Aquinas to follow. No less did Calvin and other non-Catholic Christians follow this example. Between 1542 and 1546, fifty-eight persons were executed for heresy by Calvin's authority.[12]

Jesus tells us to forgive seventy times seven. He doesn't warn us about our own safety or the safety of others, but He tells us to love one another. How can we love one another when we excommunicate, execute, or even sabotage one another? Love does not thrive on separation but rather on congregation. Let the wheat grow with the chaff.

A church which to this day runs military schools and which until recently told Catholics that it was immoral for them not to defend their country, a church which in a world history book, published for Catholic high school social studies, provides but one page in 600 on the first 300 years of the church, needs some revising.[13] A church which has invested in war industries needs to reexamine itself.[14] A church which continues to support armies, if only symbolically through its Swiss guards, needs to take a long look at itself.

Why is it that a church which has been so absolute in the area of sex, particularly divorce and abortion, is so flexible in the area of violence? The very same early Christians whom we mentioned in the earlier part of this work who absolutely supported nonviolence, spoke just as absolutely against abortion, and the church accepts their position on this type of killing. Athenagoras, Tertullian, Menucius Felix, Hippolytus, Cyprian, and Lactantius all universally condemned abortion as a violation of the commandment against killing.[15]

Thomas Merton and Pacifism

American Catholic theologian Thomas Merton, prior to his death, was coming around to war resistance, although he still did not seem to accept the early Christian application of pacifism. He looked upon it as somewhat Manichaean, and said that "the religious ambiguities in the term 'pacifism' give it implications that are somewhat less than Catholic.

. . . A Christian pacifist then becomes one who compounds his ambiguity by insisting, or at least by implying, that pacifism is an integral part of Christianity, with the evident conclusion that Christians who are not pacifist have, by that fact, apostacized from Christianity."[16] Merton said he was not referring to conscientious objectors but that pacifism takes, as a cause, a kind of faith in its own right. He defined a pacifist as one who "believes in peace so to speak as an article of faith and hence puts himself in a position of being absolutely unable to countenance any form of war, since for him to accept any war in theory or practice would be to deny his faith."[17]

It seems to me that Merton denied the witness of Maximilian and Martin of Tours. Did his description of pacifism not describe them exactly? Did not Merton know that this was their Christian way of life? He later wrote: "War was neither blessed nor forbidden by Christ. He simply stated that war belonged to the world outside the kingdom, the world outside the mystery and Spirit of Christ and that therefore for one who was seriously living in Christ, war belonged to a realm that no longer had a decisive meaning, for though the Christian was 'in the world' he was not 'of the world.' "[18] He took this position, however, on the erroneous assumption that the reason early Christians were acting this way was because they forsaw an early end to the world.[19]

This explanation of early Christian pacifism has been refuted by MacGregor, Windass, Bainton, and Cadoux among other authorities. On the whole, Merton's relaxed attitude toward Christian violence could stem from his position that "a Catholic may not hold that all war under no matter what conditions is by its very nature unjust and evil. A Catholic may not formally deny that a community has a right to defend itself by force if other means do not avail.[20]

Truly it is our task to understand the meaning of the Word. With the help of the Spirit and in dialogue with Christians this can be achieved. Although the church has spent much time on dogmatizing certain parts of Scripture, it has not spent a comparable amount of time in precisely determining the meaning of the gospel message. Relevant biblical passages on violence and nonviolence in the Scriptures should be compiled to form a base for study by Christians, the result of which hopefully would be a teaching statement by Christians to Christians on their responsibilities for peace.

Violence, Catholicism, and World War II

If Berrigan seems to seek peace through violence, his zeal against war certainly must have been in part a reaction to the almost unbelievable Catholic justification of war in the past. Gordon Zahn reported, for instance, that an American parochial school textbook assured its readers "that a soldier who dies on the battlefield earns immediate entry to heaven,"[21] and that the German Bishop Conrad Grober advised his flock before the advent of Hitler: "In her almost two thousand years of existence, the church has never yet absolved her members from military duty. . . . She has on the contrary, rejected the extreme and helpless pacifism which sees war as something forbidden and un-Christian. . . . Catholics have never left it to the judgment of the individual. . . . The final decision has been left to legitimate authority."[22]

Zahn shows us in page after page, how the German Catholic Church encouraged Germans to support the violence of their government in war. "The Catholic Church in Germany itself represented a major force for assuring conformity to the demands of the national war effort on the part of the individual German Catholic; and in assuming this role, it employed the full range of the institutional controls at its command."[23] If the German bishops had preached the Sermon on the Mount instead of continuous patriotic pronouncements on the glory of war, perhaps Hitler would never have formed his base. If Pius XI had not praised Hitler,[24] and if all the nations, not just Denmark, had supported the Jews nonviolently, perhaps fewer Jews would have died. Only forty-two Jews died in Denmark in concentration camps, mostly of natural causes, as a result of the stout-hearted nonviolent resistance utilized in Denmark in contrast to the violent resistance offered elsewhere.[25]

Danilo Dolci and Cardinal Ruffini

If we wonder why modern Catholics still resort to violence, a comparison of two contemporaries will help to point out the changing scene. One was a respected leader and professed follower of Christ, Cardinal Ruffini. The other is a man of the people, a pacifist, a doer of nonviolent works, Danilo Dolci.

Dolci has said of the Catholic Church in Italy:

> It doesn't seem to be interested in goodness for its own sake. I have never heard a priest say that one should not kill. No priest has ever said "enough" to the murders committed in this zone. The Church of Pope John XXIII interested me; but not the present one.[26]

In a conference with Cardinal Ruffini, Dolci came under fire for his stand as a conscientious objector in World War II. Ruffini said to Dolci, "If you had come to me in time you would not have lost your faith. You a Christian, who left Christianity and grew up alone. You grew up badly and made serious errors. . . . If it weren't for the Americans, we would all be under the domination of the communists."

Danilo replied, "I am against all wars. At the age of eighteen I was arrested as a conscientious objector."

Ruffini replied, "The idea of being a conscientious objector is nonsense."

Danilo: "You really believe that?"

Cardinal: "Yes."

Danilo: "Don't you believe that fundamentally Christ was a conscientious objector?"

Cardinal: "The individual cannot oppose public opinion. The individual must know that those who have power over him know more than he does. Your objections serve no purpose. He who is in charge knows what to do."[27]

Dolci, a man not far removed from God, said, "If God would take me by the ear and tell me when I am right or wrong, that would make me happy."[28]

According to Dolci's biographer, Dolci treated Cardinal Ruffini kindly, but the Cardinal "denounced Dolci as a 'publicist' in a great conspiracy to dishonor Italy. This condemnation was publicly approved by Pope Paul, and could have had the effect of encouraging his death by the Mafia."[29] If true, perhaps this is why Dolci is wary of the Catholic Church. Dolci wrote:

> During the war I saw every act of violence done, without clear reason, by people who more or less call themselves Christians. It was very difficult for me to become fully conscious of what in the depths of myself I felt to be truth and coherence. . . . When I was seven years old they had already put a gun in my hands, and in the books I was given, violence was always exalted, and praise lavished not on the one who was right but on the one who was stronger.[30]

Dolci lives today in Sicily. He remains "the criminal" and the cardinal "the saint." But it is he who practices the nonviolence of the early church. Should the modern church treat him as it has?

Because the Catholic hierarchy in general -- for example, the German bishops and Cardinal Ruffini — followed the Augustinian justification of violence, it is not difficult to foresee that the result has been more violence. Tolstoy warned us: "If we once admit the right of any man to resist by violence what he regards as evil, every other man has equally the right to resist by violence what he regards as evil."[31] And thus it is also with Catholic revolutionary violence of the type of Camillo Torres. But no type of violence is justified by the Scriptures for Christians, neither Ruffini violence, Berrigan violence, nor Torres violence, and the failure of this type of thinking is clearly a contributing cause of much of the violence in the world today. It is imperative that the church instruct the Ruffinis the Berrigans and the Torres in the true meaning of Christian nonviolence.

I do not want to leave the impression that Cardinal Ruffini or the Berrigans are totally violent Christians, or that there are no Christians living today who could be described as Catholic witnesses for pacifism and nonviolence. It is true that in interviewing Daniel Berrigan in 1968, James Finn said, "You obviously have a position which rejects violence but nevertheless see some conditions under which it may be the best alternative, at least in the minds of the people who are there presently involved."[32] But one cannot reject violence and do violence, and this seems to be what Daniel Berrigan has been preaching and doing. Of course, it all depends on how you define violence. If destroying property is not a violent act because it does not involve persons, then according to that definition, the destroyer of property is nonviolent. Daniel Berrigan does not seem to believe the destruction of property is a violent act. Apparently Dorothy Day, a Catholic pacifist of our times, does.

During the Arab-Israeli war of 1973 many looked to those who were witnesses for peace in Vietnam, and asked, Will they witness again to Christian peace and pacifism in the Middle East where it might be more difficult? The political power and persuasion of American Zionists toward the just war is a much stronger power than any held by pro-North Vietnamese sympathizers in this country. But Daniel Berrigan became one of the first anti-Vietnam war spokesman to take a position for neither the Israelis nor the Arabs but for peace in the Middle East. Berrigan emerges as a consistent "pacifist" in opposing the use of violence by governments, but apparently neither brother requires the same pacifism for those in opposition to government.

In response to a question of James Finn, Berrigan said, "And I have to separate my thinking — again, just for myself — with regard to the kind of violence that a people needs in order to become itself within a deprived nation, and the kind of violence which is allowable to the nuclear power in its international dealings. And for myself I find these are two very separate questions."[33] And Finn in a conversation with Philip Berrigan noted that Berrigan does not reject the view that violence under some circumstances might be called for.[34] Apparently the Berrigans justify the violence of the oppressed within a deprived nation but not the violence of governments. Where do the Scriptures support such a distinction? Perhaps the Berrigans would justify a Catholic who lived in the poverty of a South American country in shooting his way out of that predicament through the use of "Christian" violence. Camilo Torres, a Catholic priest turned guerrilla who finally died by the sword, is an example of this. But if the Berrigans and Camilo Torres support the violence of the oppressed, there are Catholics who do not — not because such violence is not just, but because it is not Jesus.

Contemporary Catholic Pacifists

A Catholic, Franz Jaegerstatter, gave up his life in Hitler's war for his convictions. He did not describe himself as a pacifist, but he practiced peace. Gordon Zahn wrote of his life and death in a book entitled *In Solitary Witness.*[35] Jaegerstatter believed that Hitler's war was unjust. Although his priest and other clerical authorities told him that it was not for him to decide what was a just war and what was not, he followed his convictions and was arrested. He did not resist and he was imprisoned. He was told by the Catholic authorities that it was entirely right for a German national to fight in Hitler's war in self-defense because self-defense is always an exception to violence. He was told that if he continued in his obstinate ways, he might lose his life and his family would suffer. He didn't run away. He didn't form a guerrilla band. He didn't take up the sword against Hitler. He did not resist, but followed his convictions to the end and died in Berlin in 1943. He harmed no one but remained totally nonviolent, and gave his life for his convictions. He followed Jesus' example and the Sermon on the Mount in a totally pacifistic and nonviolent way.

Probably the two leading Catholic witnesses for nonviolence in America today are Caesar Chavez and Dorothy Day. Dorothy Day had her political beginnings in the communist party in the early thirties. Her husband was a communist, but over the span of years she became disillusioned and left the party. She originated the *Catholic Worker* newspaper, and provided a Catholic social witness in competition with the communist social witness of the time. All these years Dorothy Day has been practicing nonviolence, nonresistance, and pacifism. During the war she peacefully demonstrated against all wars, and was imprisoned for her convictions. Her life has been one of voluntary poverty. She lives in a community of dedicated nonviolent Christians on a farm outside of New York and in the Bowery of New York, working on the soup lines and in hospitality houses for the poor and impoverished, the addicts and the sick, the violent and the homeless. Her witness has been quiet and virtually unpublicized, but throughout she has been a strong supporter of her church and an admirer of those Catholics who have witnessed to peace. She has been a good sister to her beloved enemies, the violent, not by adopting their ways but by giving her ways.[36]

Caesar Chavez grew up in a Mexican family of migrant workers, and wanted to do something about the horrible conditions of such third-class citizens. In the Mexican culture *machismo* is a very important characteristic relating to manliness. Many of us more waspy Americans have an idea of what this means — that the man must demonstrate that he is a man by some aggressive "manly" act. The Indians used to send their young bucks out alone to conquer the wilderness with their bow and arrow. Today university fraternities try to discover manliness through their "hell" weeks. The army talks about separating the men from the boys.

In the Mexican environment this is a very important characteristic and may be demonstrated by the use of physical violence. Chavez rejected this ethic. He has given up violence and has truly become a man without it. His concern is for the improvement of the social conditions of the migrant worker. When he obtained his first contract for his followers in the grape boycott several years ago, he was asked whether he could have accomplished that feat in less than eight years. And he said yes, but not without violence.

But resorting to violence would have been wrong. Chavez felt, so he waited for eight years to accomplish with non-violence what might have been achieved in two. Chavez sums up his belief in the following words:

> When we are really honest with ourselves we must admit that our lives are all that really belongs to us. So it is how we use our lives that determines what kind of men we are. It is my deepest belief that only by giving our lives do we find life. I am convinced that the truest act of courage, the strongest act of manliness is to sacrifice ourselves for others in a totally non-violent struggle for justice. To be a man is to suffer for others. God help us to be men.[37]

There are men and women among the cloth who also have experienced the delight of the nonviolent witness of Jesus. In India, Mother Teresa of Calcutta and her followers try to bring love and comfort to those who are homeless and dying in the streets. Everyday she "walks the extra mile" with her sisters, picking up diseased and dying bodies left in the street gutters to die. She brings them to the infirmary where they are washed, nursed, and watched until their last hour.

Mother Teresa's ministry of Christian nonviolence is not in the political arena although it may very well be that politics helped to create the deplorable conditions in which she finds her creatures. Those who die in the streets may be there because of some social or political injustice which established a system so cruel and unloving that those who never had a chance are left to die. Mother Teresa fights the system in her own way nonviolently by giving what she has — her love to these people. She does not resist the government. She does not demonstrate against it directly, but she does provide a Christian witness to all "Caesars" who would allow such conditions to exist within the confines of their borders, and to all "Caesars" outside the confines of those borders who do not help the people of less fortunate countries who are in need.[38]

In South America Catholic Cardinal Dom Helder Camara shows the nonviolent way to revolutionary change. An outspoken critic of violence, he can sympathize with a Camilo Torres, the ex-Catholic priest and self-styled guerrilla who undertook to use violence to eradicate the injustices and violence of institutional government. But he provides an alternative witness to Torres in South America, a Christian witness built on a totally nonviolent activism.[39] And he looks to the charismatic Cardinal Suenens as the leading Catholic prelate of our times. Suenens combines the evangelicalism of Pentecost with the humanism of peace, a rare combination in the church.

Closer to home is John L. McKenzie, S. J. McKenzie is a leading Catholic biblical scholar, a former teacher at DePaul University and a visiting professor at the University of Chicago Divinity School, the first Roman Catholic priest to hold this position. In an interview with James Finn in 1968 McKenzie shared these thoughts on war and violence:

> I think that war is essentially irrational. And immoral. It's essentially irrational because violence, by definition, is not a solution of human questions. . . . I have not had any use for the just-war theory for about ten years. And it just came all of a sudden — there was nothing to it. It's a kind of theoretical and totally impractical moral thinking that moralists just like to engage in every now and then. It has no reference to the real world at all . . . and so I put the ethics of the just-war in almost the same boat with the ethics of the just adultery or the just murder.[40]

McKenzie sounds a lot like Richard McSorley, another

Jesuit who teaches at Georgetown University in Washington, D.C. McSorley, in a small book called *Kill for Peace?*[41] shows the immorality of nuclear technology and Christian violence and the combination of both which is leading us close to a holocaust. In Memphis, Tennessee, Catholic Bishop Dozier in his first pastoral message called his flock to the study of peace, and his efforts in this regard have been in contrast to the general tenor of his church. These Catholics are publicly known, but there are many Catholics who are not known at all who have witnessed to and practiced the teachings of Jesus and the Sermon on the Mount.

Even though establishment Protestantism has not espoused pacifism, Protestantism has its legitimate pacifistic wing. After the Reformation, Protestantism broke into Lutheranism, Calvinism, and Anabaptism, and growing out of the Anabaptist movement were the pacifistic historic peace churches. Although these have been a small group of witnesses, the witness has been felt. But until recently a Catholic could not be a conscientious objector because his church had only one position on war and violence. Since Vatican II, because of the actions of Pope John and other Catholic priests and lay pacifists, there has now grown an alternative to justified violence — the pacifistic alternative.

Perhaps one day it will no longer be an alternative but "the Way."

Modern Protestant Trends

Thus far we have concentrated on current aspects of violence and nonviolence as they relate to Roman Catholicism. This is not to say that Protestantism is without a modern history in this regard. However, because Roman Catholicism gave birth to the Christian doctrine of justified violence, in effect plagiarizing it from Rome's Cicero, we have not emphasized the role of Protestantism in this regard. Also, Protestantism has not spoken with the authoritative hierarchical voice on this issue as would a church with the authoritative structure of Roman Catholicism.

A complete post-Reformation history of the impact of violence and nonviolence in Catholicism and Protestantism is not our intention. However, paralleling the Roman Catholic Church of the modern era, major Protestant spokesmen have tended to support the just-war theory. Some say that Reinhold Niebuhr has probably influenced twentieth-century American theology more than any other individual.[42] And Niebuhr above all has been greatly influenced by Augustine.[43] Niebuhr, Paul Ramsey, Paul Tillich, and Billy Graham are typical of orthodox, liberal, and conservative Protestantism's voice favoring justified violence. Ramsey has been particularly instrumental in justifying the use of violence as a means of bringing "peace."[44] Tillich asked us to find a way between pacifism and militarism.

Neither Niebuhr, Tillich, nor Ramsey could be described as activists in the style of conservative radio preacher Carl MacIntire who has personally led young and old alike in anticommunist parades across the country. One of his young followers advised me that as a good Christian it was my duty to kill communists for Christ! MacIntire's group, however, is not typical of all Protestant activity in this regard.

Lay Protestant groups, until recently, far surpassed their Roman Catholic counterparts in pacifistic action. This is also true of individual Protestant pacifists such as A. J. Muste. The Fellowship of Reconciliation and other similar groups were formed primarily by Protestants and have been in existence since the first World War.

Niebuhr states that pacifists have been misled into believing that "man is essentially good at some level of his being," and that "a theology which thus fails to come to grips with the tragic fact of sin is radical."[45] He believes that the failure of the pacifist to recognize this evil in human nature creates a confidence in nonresistance as a method of overcoming evil. Niebuhr's argument seems to be that since we're so sinful, nonviolence can't work. Therefore, it's unchristian. He concludes that "there's not the slightest support in the Scripture for this doctrine of nonviolence."[46] Niebuhr is essentially typical of liberal orthodox Protestant theology which does not see nonresistance, enemy loving, and pacifism as integral to Christianity.

However, Protestants themselves remain split on the issue of Christian peace as do Catholics. Lutherans are as far removed from Mennonites on this issue as Catholics are among themselves.

The 1971 Catholic Synod said that "in certain cases the Christian message is neither known nor put into practice by the community of the faithful."[47] What kind of witness can Christians expect to give to non-Christians in the world if we only love those who love us? Jesus said that even the pagans do as much.

All who follow Christ's footsteps by resisting not the wicked man, turning the other cheek, and loving their enemies are "successful" witnesses whether their physical bodies are tortured or killed. But for those who have a tendency to be swayed by the fruits they can see, we can say with confidence, that nonviolence has indeed worked here on earth in many instances when on those rare occasions Christians have attempted to follow the instruction of Christ.

CHAPTER 9

Violence or Nonviolence? No King but Jesus!

Although the institutional church may not have preached a proper Christian example, many individual Christians have practiced it. Even some who do not call themselves Christians such as Gandhi, have practiced an ethic of peace. He lived and died nonviolence with God's name on his final breath. An admirer of Jesus,[1] Gandhi was a powerful influence for good. So is his Indian follower Vinoba Bhave. A long list of individuals who practiced nonviolence could be compiled, including Protestants such as Toyohiko Kagawa in Japan and Albert Luthuli in Africa, to name only a few. Many others have already been mentioned. People such as the Universalist minister Adin Ballou in America, and Leo Tolstoy in Russia in the previous century, paved the way by their example for the actions of Gandhi and for the nonviolent work of Martin Luther King, Jr.

This modern Martin led the nonviolent movement for black civil rights in America. King said:

> We will be guided by the highest principles of law and order. . . . Our method will be that of persuasion, not coercion. We will only say to the people, "Let your conscience be your guide." Our actions must be guided by the deepest principles of our Christian faith. Love must be our regulating ideal. Once again we must hear the words of Jesus echoing across the centuries: "Love your enemies, bless those that curse you, and pray for them that dispitefully use you." If we fail to do this, our protest will end up as a meaningless drama on the stage of history, and its memory will be shrouded with the ugly garments of shame. In spite of the mistreatment that we have confronted, we must not become bitter and end up by hating our white brothers. As Booker T. Washington said, "Let no man pull you down so low to make you hate him. . . ." If you will protest courageously and yet with dignity and Christian love, when the history books are written in the future generations, the historians will have cause to say, "There lived a great people — a black people — who injected new meaning and dignity into the veins of civilization." This is our challenge and our overwhelming responsibility.[2]

King did not speak in the abstract. When his home was bombed and some of his followers called for retaliation, he said, "I want you to go home and put down your weapons. We cannot solve this problem through retaliatory violence. We must meet violence with non-violence. Remember the words of Jesus: 'He who lives by the sword will perish by the sword.' We must love our white brothers no matter what they do to us. We must make them know that we love them."[3]

Martin Luther King had something to say about the church also. "The Church has not always lived up to its prophetic calling. It is not enough for religious institutions to be active in the realm of ideas. They must move out into the area of love. Man-made laws assure justice. But a higher law provides love. . . . If the churches would free themselves from the shackles of the deadening status quo . . . they will enkindle the imagination of mankind and fire the soul of men, embuing them with a glowing and ardent love for truth and justice. I am sure that this alliance of conscience would only be a sign of the coming of the kingdom."[4]

In his book, *Strength from Love,* Martin Luther King wrote on the love of enemy:

> A third reason why we should love our enemies is that love is the only force capable of transforming an enemy into a friend. We never get rid of an enemy by meeting hate with hate; we get rid of an enemy by getting rid of enmity. By its very nature, hate destroys and tears down; by its very nature love creates and builds up. Love transforms with redemptive power. . . . We must hasten to say that these are not the only reasons why we should love our enemies. An even more basic reason why we are commanded to love is expressed explicitly in Jesus' words, "Love your enemies . . . that you may be children of your Father which is in heaven."[5]

King reminded us that Napoleon Bonaparte was reported to have said, "Alexander, Caesar, Charlemagne, and I have built great empires. But upon what did they depend? They depended on force. But centuries ago, Jesus started an empire that was built on love, and even to this day millions will die for him."[6]

King was a disciplined man whose personal habits included daily meditation on the teachings and life of Jesus, daily prayer that he might be used by God to help set all men free, sacrifice of personal comfort for the larger cause, observation with both friend and foe of the ordinary rules of courtesy, refraining from the violence of fist, tongue, or heart, and striving always to be in good spiritual and bodily health.[7]

Martin Luther King concluded his life by saying,

> I do not know what will happen now. We've got some difficult days ahead but that really doesn't matter to me now. Because I've been to the mountaintop, I won't mind. Like anyone else I would like to live a long life. Longevity has its place, but I'm not concerned about that now. I just want to do God's will. And he's allowed me to go up to the mountain and I've looked over and I've seen the Promised Land. So I'm happy tonight, I'm not worried about anything. I'm not fearing any man. Mine eyes have seen the glory of the coming of the Lord.[8]

And Martin Luther King left us the following day, perhaps saying in a voice we no longer hear, "Free at last. Free at last. God, almighty, I am free at last."

Some say Martin Luther King failed. This argument assumes that the nonviolent way of life is under the bondage of material success. It is not. Martin Luther King did succeed not only as a person but as a public figure. Many changes have been wrought in society as the result of his nonviolent direct action.

Immanuel Kant said that the most dangerous thing is when violence meets with success because success seems to legitimize violence. The converse is true also. When nonviolence meets with failure, there are those who say that only violence will succeed. Christian nonviolence is not concerned with material success. Those who practice it do so not to be "successful" but because it is right.

The Failure of Violence

For those who think in terms of material success it is well to point out that violence has brought us to where we are today. Does violence really succeed? The National Commission on Causes and Prevention of Violence published their official report in June 1969 asking that question. Their findings indicate that when those who use violence are sufficiently dedicated, they will be successful in achieving their aims. Those in government hold essentially the same belief, that is "that sufficient use of public violence will deter private violence."[9] Both the right and left, the liberal and the conservative, the radical and the reactionary, the church and the state, black and white have favored violence on the grounds that it succeeds.

But is not the so-called success of violence really only a short period of temporary tranquility? If violence were actually successful, we would have experienced a permanent peace after the first use of violence. This has not been the case.

Whether successful or not, violence is costly. Richard McSorley points out in his striking book *Kill for Peace?* that "the United States spends over $650,000,000 a year on chemical biological research. This is almost four times what the country spends on cancer research."[10]

The lure of committing violence is a temptation for many. Pope Urban II launched a crusade for a war which would heal and unify. He supposed that the separation of the Eastern and Western churches could be healed by force and divided Christendom reunited. So he went to the aid of the emperor in the East against the foe of all Christendom, the Arab infidel. His crusade to Palestine began in political expediency and ended in violent failure.[11]

Roland Bainton, in his book *Christian Attitudes Towards War and Peace,* points out an example of Roman violence and its failure to achieve desired ends.[12] During the time of the Roman Emperor Valens, the Visigoths, endangered by the Huns, requested permission to bring their families within the borders of the Roman Empire. Totaling over one million people, they had become Christian. The Emperor Valens promised their leader, Fritigern, admission. He came over the Danube but Rome did not honor their agreement and they were corralled like cattle and fed only dead dogs. To obtain food the price for each dog was a child sold to slavery. Fritigern's guard was murdered by the Romans, and eventually the Visigoths broke loose and terrorized Thrace. The Emperor Valens challenged them in battle and died together with over half of his army. It was only *then* that a Spanish general named Theodosius restored order by granting the settlement promised by the Emperor Valens to the Visigoths. Bainton suggests that if Rome had dealt nonviolently with her adversary, the barbarian invasions might have continued to be a controlled imigration. We see the evil of resorting to violence and how engaging in violence becomes counterproductive.

Shortly before the Reformation, Erasmus mused over the folly of war. He said, "Consider the cost of it all. In order to prevent the enemy from leaving his towns one must sleep for months outside of one's own. New walls could be built for less than is required to batter down old ones. When all the damage is taken into account, the most brilliant success is not worth the trouble."[13]

Or consider these remarks: 'How then is peace to be secured? Not by royal marriages, but by cleansing the human heart. Why should one born in the bogs of Ireland seek by some alliance to rule over the East Indies. Let a king recall that to improve his realm is better than to increase his territory. Let him buy peace. The cheapest war would be more expensive. Let him invite the arbitration of learned men, abbots, and bishops. Let the clergy absent themselves from silly parades and refuse Christian burial to those who die in battle."[14] Who said these mighty words?

Not a peaceful saint but a mighty warrior, perhaps disillusioned with his failures of violence, Henry VIII.

What appears to be the successful use of violence at the end of a war may truly be only the seeds of new violence. For example, to win the Boer war the English were required to construct concentration camps for Boer civilians. After the war, peace and home rule were granted to the Boers. But the outcome of the war for the native was apartheid.[15]

Everyone has a just cause to wage violence. Even Hitler claimed to be justified in his use of violence. His defeat was supposed to bring peace to the world and harmony to civilization. Hitler was a tyrant who spied on his own, practiced prejudice against his enemies, and built up the greatest war machine the world had ever known, and justified his actions by claiming he would stop atheistic communism. His conquerors have now honored him by imitation. America has built up the greatest war machine the world has ever known to fight the same "eternal enemy," Russia, while fighting racial minorities within. Did America really "win" the war? And with our own spying in Watergate we are all too familiar.

In World War II the atomic bomb brought an end to the war in Japan, but what happened, asked Mahatma Gandhi to the souls of those who dropped the bomb? Those who do violence even in a righteous cause may destroy their own spirit. Those men who engaged in the violence of World War II may be in part responsible for the violence of the ghettos that plague us now or the violence of the children who grew up fatherless during the war years.

The French resistance to Nazi Germany was aimed at creating a free and just republic, says Jacques Ellul. However, he records that "in 1945 the same resisters massacred 45,000 people in Algeria and in 1947 they massacred almost

100,000 in Madagascar."[16] Arnold Toynbee summed it up well when he said that war has been the proximate cause of the downfall of every civilization which is known to have deteriorated.

The National Commission on the Causes and Prevention of Violence admits that the Indian population of the United States was so small when the white men arrived here that there was plenty of room for the expansion of white settlements. The Indians could have easily been reimbursed for the land needed for occupation by the white man because the economic resources of the white settlers were so great.[17] But instead the goddess of violence was honored and for hundreds of years war and violence ensued to the grief of Indians and whites alike.

Christopher Columbus was received graciously by the people of Tainos on the Island of San Salvador. They presented him with gifts and treated him peacefully. Columbus was so impressed he wrote the king and queen of Spain saying, "So tractable, so peaceable are these people that I swear to your majesties there is not in the world a better nation. They love their neighbors as themselves and their discourses are so sweet and gentle, and accompanied with a smile; and though it is sure they are naked yet their manners are decorous and praiseworthy." According to Dee Brown and his monumental book, ***Bury My Heart at Wounded Knee***, this was taken as a sign of weakness and heathenism. But Columbus was convinced that the people should be "made to work, sew, and do all that is necessary and to adopt our ways."[18] So violence was inflicted upon the Indian, and the Indian returned the same in kind. Is violence successful?

Granted, warfare is a profitable industry, a lucrative business. First we have a soldier, then a supplier, then a profiteer. In Julius Caesar's time it cost 56¢ to kill an enemy;

in the Vietnam War it cost the United States $110,000 for every death. That $110,000 went into the pockets of the manufacturers of clothes, machinery, and war weapons. War is an economic waste for the masses, but for some companies and businesses it is tremendously profitable.[19]

In fact, violence does not achieve much of anything except to spawn still more violence. Why were the James brothers admired? The James brothers were former Confederate guerrillas who learned to kill in war. After the war they could do no wrong. To Southern sympathizers and grange minded farmers their repeated robberies of banks and railroads were exactly what those institutions deserved.[20]

When we learn to kill so readily in war, we do not stop in peace. The feud that the McCoys and the Hatfields engaged in can be traced directly to their involvement in the Civil War.[21] The Report of the National Commission on the Causes and Prevention of Violence states that the philosophy that the end justifies the means became the keynote of revolutionary violence in America, and since that time Americans have never been loath to employ the most unremitting violence in the interests of any cause deemed to be a good one.[22] No one, no community, no nation has ever successfully used violence without being hurt in the process. We should have learned by now that violence begets violence, not success!

The Spirit of Nonviolence

When will we be ready to try nonviolence and give it a real chance? Some lonely souls have attempted to live nonviolently in the past.

Adin Ballou, a pacifist Christian minister of the last century, practiced nonviolence for many years, and was aware of many instances of the success of nonviolence in the relationships between whites and Indians in colonial America.

Ballou reports that the Indians were asked why they did not attack the Shakers. They replied, "We warriors meddle with a peaceable people? That people we know will not fight. It would be a disgrace to hurt such a people." The Indians left a white feather at the Shaker's home to indicate their sign of peace.[23] Apparently the Indians, illiterate and savage according to the white man, understood the great spiritual movement of nonviolence better than many white men do today.

The Indian also had the opportunity to understand the Quakers. The Indians came with tomahawks and found no guns among the Quakers, only peace. They found that the Quakers worshiped the Great Spirit and the spirit in the Indians' heart said, "Dont hurt them."[24] Quaker Pennsylvania coexisted for seventy years in peace with the Indians, Ballou reports. It never lost a man, woman, or child to the Indians, although there was no militia or organized defense. "After the seventy years, the legislature voted for war . . . became subject to the militia. The Quakers resigned their positions in the legislature and war and violence came to Pennsylvania."[25]

Ballou tells of an instance in Europe in the Tyrol. Invading soldiers looking for the enemy found only people working. The soldiers asked, "Where are your soldiers?" The people replied, "We have none." The soldiers said, "But we came to take your town. Is there nobody here to fight?" The townspeople replied, "No, we're all Christians." The soldiers replied, "It is impossible to take such a town," and they left.[26]

War may have more to do with pride than with property and possessions. When the enemy is nonresistant, the aggressor tends to lose his interest in overcoming him. This is psychologically the same pattern which exists when a bully refuses to hit a man with glasses. There is no victory in that. Warriors demand victory first, and those who will not fight will not provide a victory for those who wish to vanquish. "Something in our heart makes us unwilling to fight where resistance is not offered," Ballou observed. "It seems mean and dastardly. A man can't work himself up to it. He is ashamed. It takes away the glory and excitement. It would constitute cold-blooded murder."[27]

Hans DeBoer, a German pacifist, went to Kenya determined to talk to the leaders of the Mau Mau. Everyone told him that if he went into the Mau Mau country he would not come back with his head on. He consulted an American Quaker who had been in the land some twenty years. The advice was "Young man, I wouldn't do it if I were you. One should not tempt God."[28]

Bainton reports, however, that

> DeBoer nevertheless went entirely unarmed. After some two hours of walking, as he was approaching the first settlement two natives in remnants of European dress accosted him in English asking, "Are you Mr. DeBoer?" The Quaker friend who had counseled him not to go had in fact contacted the Mau Mau. DeBoer was able to have a conference with one of the leaders to whom he deplored alike the violence of the Mau Mau and of the whites urging instead negotiations. The Negro replied that if the whites would come unarmed to talk, no blood would flow. The Negroes desired only freedom and a right to their own land, and they were not lusting to murder all of the whites.[29]

Bainton reports this incidence as significant for two reasons: (1) the Quakers were able to keep lines of communication open during this conflict, and (2) a man of his own free will went unarmed among the Mau Mau and impressed them so much they gave him their courtesy. Disarmament and nonviolence might truly revolutionize the world behavior.

Danilo Dolci, the Italian reformer and idealist mentioned

in a previous chapter, decried the misery of the poor in Sicily, moved there, and devoted his life to fighting poverty. In 1956 he led a strike in which several hundred unemployed Sicilians, protesting a lack of work, followed Dolci and repaired a long neglected road on a voluntary basis with no promise of pay. Dolci and others were arrested and convicted but the court, when sentencing him, expressed appreciation of the high moral value of this action. Critics have said that the only people who can really practice nonviolence are the ones who are well-off and can afford to do it. Imagine Dolci and his impoverished followers deciding to perform a strike in reverse, striking their own jobs but using that time to repair a long neglected road on a voluntary basis with no promise of pay. The movement was successful, the strike was ended, the job regained, and later Dolci and his companions built a dam in much the same way.

But one need not be a radical to employ nonviolence successfully. Individuals who operate within the system, such as the late Dag Hammarskjöld have demonstrated the effectiveness of nonviolent action. One of many examples concerns a Hammarskjöld visit to Chou En-lai to plead for the release of eleven airmen held by the Chinese after the conclusion of the Korean War. After the visit, the Chinese embassy in Stockholm asked for the date of Hammerskjöld's birthday. On July 29, 1955, while he was celebrating his fiftieth birthday, he received a cable from the foreign minister of China announcing that the United States airmen were being released.[30]

The cease-fire which emerged from Hammarskjöld's final trip to the Congo is another example of the practice of nonviolence. Hammarskjöld flew into the Congo to meet the insurgents rather than meeting them on neutral ground. He felt that by meeting the enemy he loved on their own ground, he would show his respect for them. This was recognized and two days after his death, a cease-fire took place. After his death in an air crash it was noted that next to the table by the bed where he spent his last night were two books, the *Imitation of Christ* by Thomas á Kempis and the Gospels.[31]

In his treatise, *Pacifism in the United States,* Peter Brock tells the story of a Quaker and the Indians. The Quaker was working in his field. Indians saw him and called him. He went to them. They told him they had no quarrel with the Quakers "for they were a quiet peaceable people and hurt nobody and that therefore none should hurt them." But they said "that the Presbyterians in these parts had taken away their lands, and some of their lives, and would now, if they could, destroy all the Indians."[32] Brock also tells about another Quaker living nearby who decided to carry a gun. He was shot and killed by Indians as he went to work along with a second Quaker who was unarmed and unharmed by them. When the Indians learned that the man that they had killed was a Quaker, they seemed upset and sorry, but they said it was the fault of the Quaker for carrying a gun. They knew Quakers would not fight or do any harm. When they saw the gun they took the Quaker for an enemy.[33] According to Brock, "No Friend was known to have been attacked or killed by the Indian raiders."[34]

Many other examples of successful nonviolence have been recorded through the pages of history. Pitirim Sorokin points out the power of love in taming war and violence. The Emperor Asoka was so shaken by the violent results of his "successful" wars that he decided to replace his war policies with peace policies. He constructed orphanages and schools, eliminating injustice, reducing misery, and helping neighboring nations. And peace came for over seventy years foreshadowing William Penn's holy experiment in Quaker Pennsylvania.[35]

One of the leading books on nonviolence, *The Power of Non-violence*, by Richard Gregg, lists numerous additional examples for those who would like to expand on this short summary.[36]

There remains unanswered, however, the challenge that if we had practiced nonviolence prior to World War II, Hitler would not have been stopped. We've already asked whether in fact Hitler was stopped or whether we have become Hitlerians by using his means to bring an end to his methods. Six million Jews were killed in spite of the violence of World War II. Gandhi and King have written that there would have been ways to avert World War II through nonviolence. If every Christian had practiced the teaching of the Sermon on the Mount whether German, English, or American there would have been no such war, just as there would be no war in Ireland today if such were the case. Hitler came to power with the support of Christian political parties. Nonviolent civil disobedience on the part of all Christian Germans would have prevented Adolf Hitler from ever engaging in the type of terror which he brought to Germany and the world. Later, it seemed difficult to prevent Hitler through nonviolence. Even so, many Christians refused to practice violence to prevent Hitler's violence.

Danish citizens, almost to a person, wore the Jewish armbands so that they could not be distinguished from Jews who were obliged to wear such a band. Fewer Jews were killed from Denmark than any other place in Europe. Is there some relationship between the nonviolent civil disobedience the Danish used in support of the Jews, and the changing of the hearts and minds of the German soldiers occupying that country so that fewer Jews were killed and fewer Jews were shipped out of Denmark into concentration camps to die?

Tertullian answered the question on how Hitler could have been stopped by the example of nonviolent German Christians. Tertullian in preaching to the "Reich" of that day, Rome, said:

> We are but of yesterday, and already we have filled all your world; cities, islands, fortresses, towns, marketplaces, the camp itself, tribes, companies, the palace, the senate, the forum. We have left you nothing but your temples only! We can match the numbers of your armies; and from one province we shall come to be many. For what war would we not be fit and eager, even if of unequal strength, when we are so willing to be slain, if it were not that according to our discipline, it is better to be killed than to kill?
>
> Unarmed and without rebellion but simply as dissenters we could carry on the contest against you, by merely separating ourselves from you in ill-will. If such a force as we are were to desert you for some remote corner of the world, the very loss of so many citizens of whatever kind would cause your empire to blush for shame, and vengeance would be had by that very forsaking.
>
> Without doubt you would be frightened at your loneliness, at the silence of things, and at that certain stupor as of a dead world. You would have to seek for someone whom you might govern, and you would have left to you more enemies than citizens. As it is, you have fewer enemies because of the multitude of Christians; almost every citizen in nearly every city in which Christians are found. But you prefer to call us enemies of the human race rather than enemies of human error.[37]

We end our discussion on the "successes" of nonviolence by mentioning a great little king named Ethelred the Unready. Ethelred would appear on an English list of kings just before the usual list begins with Edward I. He ruled part of England at the time of the Viking invasions and although he was not king of all kings, as no one was until Edward I, he was probably the most powerful king of any part of England at that time.

The Vikings had invaded England many times and were invading again, and he was asked as the king to defend the realm from bloodshed. But Ethelred had been working to educate his people and he asked himself whether it would not be better to spend the money on education rather than on war. Foregoing all the trappings of the heroes of those times and our times, he decided to offer money to the invaders as ransom for their invasion, bloodshed, and conquering. His young son, the prince, disagreed heartily and asked how else he could prove his manhood in war if Ethelred paid them off. But Ethelred persisted and paid them off. He lost face, he saved lives, and used the saved money to educate the saved lives. The English averted the war and peace reigned under Ethelred. Some will argue that this account is apochraphal while others find the message of the story all too believable.

The Future

Martin Luther King, Dag Hammarskjöld, and others wanted to do God's will. Do we? It is time for us as members of Christian churches to lay down our weapons physically, to admit our mistaken dependence on violence in the past, and to support those isolated apostles of Christian nonresistance and peacemaking throughout the world. It is time to follow the Spirit and the words of Christ and the Scriptures in practicing peace as a means, not only as an end. George Fox, Menno Simons, Alexander Mack of the historic peace churches on the one hand, and the works of Dorothy Day, Caesar Chavez, Mother Teresa, and the pacifistic early church fathers, Athenagoras, Irenaeus, Cyprian, Maximilian, Martin of Tours on the other, urge us on. With

Tolstoy we say, You have chosen violence for thousands of years. Why not try its alternative again? The church nonviolent in the catacombs, brought peace to the world. Why not now?

The Catholic Church has persevered in teaching the truth in respect to the nature of Jesus as both God and man, but it has slackened in respect to the Christian nature of man. We ask ourselves why there is so much violence in the world. We observe that Christian churches reinforce the justification of violence by communists and dictators by supporting violence themselves.

It is time for the Christian churches of the world to lay down their material weapons of violence and take up the spiritual armor Paul talks about. Francis told us, "You do not know what you have not practiced." How can we practice it?

First, we can start by publicly confessing our violent errors of the past to the world because it was the world we polluted with them. Since the fourth century, the majority of Christians have been poor witnesses of the peace and nonviolence of Christ, and the least we can do is admit:

(1) That we had more faith in Constantine's arms for security and protection than in God, our Creator who controls wind and waves, planets and people, and who counts every hair on our heads.

(2) That we had more faith in Augustine's words that we could kill for just causes than in the Word who lived and died for us, whose words very clearly tell us to love our enemies, turn the other cheek, and do good to those who hate us.

(3) That we had more faith in our worldly methods, such as burning at the stake to rid ourselves of heretics, than in Jesus' methods who told us to leave those alone

who refuse to receive or listen — to shake the dust from our feet and go to the next place.

(4) That we had more faith in Pope Urban II's words to fight in the Crusades against the Muslims instead of faith in Jesus who said He is the Way, the Truth, and the Life and that His kingdom is not of this world.

(5) That we had more faith in nuclear weapons and physical might so that we became lukewarm in our faith in the might and power of God. We lost our trust in Him and clung to worldly power. We forgot to pray for those who persecuted us and we forgot to do good to those who hated us. We forgot that God can do all things.

Second, we can ask forgiveness from those to whom we have done violence — individuals, churches, and nations. We could start by asking forgiveness from the following:

(1) The Muslims for having killed their people during the Crusades; the Indians and Jews for having persecuted them.

(2) The nations for not teaching the peace gospel of Christ.

(3) The members of our church for not having taught the peace gospel as Jesus preached it.

Third, we can call upon the Holy Spirit for the strength, courage, and faith to move mountains so that we *will* carry out His command to teach all nations and to love everyone in those nations. Then in good conscience, we may join Justin Martyr in saying: "We who were filled with war and mutual slaughter and every wickedness have each of us in all the world changed our weapons of war . . . swords into plows, and spears into agricultural implements." Only then will we be able to truly proclaim with Maximilian, "My arms are with the Lord. I cannot fight for any earthly consideration. I am now a Christian."

Fourth, we must teach. All Christian educational, religious, and counseling facilities, seminaries, schools, and churches should teach the peace gospel as the only alternative to implement Christian peace to young and old, cleric and laymen alike. Let us become the good witnesses we should for Christ. Let us make Jesus our King. Let us forever eradicate the claim: "We have no King but Caesar!" And then —

Let Our Violence End

Notes

Introduction

1. Paul Rosenweig (ed.), *The Wisdom of Tolstoy* (New York: Philosophical Library, 1968).
2. Tolstoy used a version of the Bible which translated Matthew 5:39 as "resist not evil." The Revised Standard Version carries a more accurate translation "Do not resist one who is evil." *The New American Bible* puts it, "Offer no resistance to injury"; *The New English Bible,* "Do not set yourself against the man who wrongs you," and *The Jerusalem Bible,* "Offer the wicked man no resistance."
3. By any standard, the early Christians were nonviolent, nonresistant, and pacifistic. As I use these terms in this context, the essence of nonviolence is the negative act of refraining from violence because of love of one's enemies, coupled with an affirmative act of love or justice. Gandhi and King would be examples of those who practiced nonviolence and resisted injustice to establish social and political justice. The essence of nonresistance is the negative act of refraining from violence because of love of one's enemies, coupled with an affirmative act of love for God and for one another. It is a type of nonviolence which concentrates not so much on the obtaining of social justice as on the giving of love to the unjust by walking the extra mile with one's enemy or by giving to those in need even when they do not in justice deserve it. The essence of pacifism is the negative act of refraining from participation in war and is inspired by the virtue of love or justice. Of course acts of nonviolence, nonresistance, or pacifism which do not have as their inspiration love or justice may simply be passivism motivated by cowardice, egoism, hedonism.

   Violence, like nonviolence is not passive, but unlike nonviolence it is a destructive force which is directed against human life, physcially, psychologically, and environmentally. Physically, it justifies the destruction of human life by war, rebellion, riot, revolt, capital punishment, abortion, infanticide, or parricide. Psychologically it is motivated by hate to discriminate because of color, race, religion, sex, nationality, age, employment, education, status, or some other arbitrary classification. Environmentally, it justifies the destruction of property and possessions whether it be clean air and water or draft boards and cards.

   For those who are nonviolent, there are no such justifications for the use of violence against one's person or property, or against the oppressed, or even against the oppressor. One who calls himself nonviolent and who discriminates in its use, whether he be of the establishment or against the establishment cannot be said to be nonviolent. He has simply replaced one form of violence with another.

No King but Caesar?

Chapter One

1. Walter M. Abbott (ed.), *The Documents of Vatican II* (New York: America Press, 1966), p. 293.
2. *Ibid.*, p. 293.
3. *Ibid.*, p. 293.
4. *Ibid.*, pp. 29, 30.
5. *Ibid.*, p. 295.
6. *Ibid.*, p. 297.
7. *Ibid.*, p. 291.
8. *Ibid.*, p. 227.
9. Eileen Egan (ed.), *The War That Is Forbidden: Peace Beyond Vatican II* (New York: American Pax Association, no date), pp. 66, 67.
10. Albert Martin (ed.), *War and the Christian Conscience* (Chicago: Henry Regnery Co., 1971), pp. 40-42.
11. G. H. C. Macgregor, *The New Testament Basis of Pacifism* (Nyack, N.Y.: Fellowship Publishing Co., 1954), p. 89.

Chapter Two

1. Cecil John Cadoux, *The Early Church and the World* (Edinburgh, Scotland: T. & T. Clark Publishing Co., 1925), p. 30, fn. 5.
2. Hans Windisch, *The Meaning of the Sermon on the Mount* (Philadelphia: Westminister Press, 1951), pp. 168-172.
3. Cadoux, *op. cit.*, p. 427. In addition to Windisch and Cadoux, two of the finest books on the relationship of the teaching of Jesus and nonviolence are *Jesus and Human Conflict* (Scottdale, Pa.: Herald Press, 1959) by Henry Fast, and *War and the Gospel*, 1962, by Jean Lasserre of the same publisher.
4. D. Martyn Lloyd-Jones, *Studies in the Sermon on the Mount* (Richmond, Va.: John Knox Press, 1964).
5. John H. Yoder, *The Politics of Jesus* (Grand Rapids, Mich.: Wm. B. Eerdmans Publishing Co., 1972), pp. 211, 214.
6. Lactantius, *The Divine Institutes*, Book 6, Chap. 20; Windass, pp. 8-9, *Infra*, chap. 5, fn. 15.
7. Lloyd-Jones, *op. cit.*, p. 278.
8. James Ross (ed.), *The War Within* (New York: Sheed & Ward, 1971), pp. 97, 101.
9. James T. Fisher and Lowell S. Hawley, *A Few Buttons Missing* (New York: J. B. Lippincott Company, 1951), pp. 273, 274.
10. Raymond I. Cramer, *The Psychology of Jesus and Mental Health*, copyright 1959 by Cowman Publications, Inc., pp. 73, 74. For an interesting explanation of biblical editing in the King James Version, where the words "without a cause" are added after "whosoever is angry with his brother," see Walter M. Abbott *et al*, *The Bible Reader* (London: Geoffrey Chadman, Ltd., 1969), p. 655.
11. *Ibid.*, p. 189.
12. *Ibid.*, p. 231. See also Price, "What Hate Can Do to You" (St. Paul, Minn.: *Catholic Digest*, March 1971), pp. 89-92.

Chapter Three

1. Summers and Howard (eds.), *Law, Its Nature, Functions, and Limits* (Engle-

woods Cliffs, N.J.: Prentice-Hall, 1972), p. 534.
2. Vernard Eller, *King Jesus, Manual of Arms for the 'Armless* (Nashville: Abingdon Press, 1973).
3. *Ibid.*, p. 73.
4. *Ibid.*, p. 72.
5. *Ibid.*, p. 106. Compare this "fighting" with that described by Tertullian, *Infra*, chap. 5, fn. 32.
6. *Ibid.*, p. 113, 114.

Chapter Five

1. Kirsopp Lake (ed.), *The Apostolic Fathers*, Vol. 1 (London: Harvard Press, 1970), p. 309.
2. G. H. C. Macgregor, *The New Testament Basis of Pacifism* (Nyack, N.Y.: Fellowship Pub., 1954), p. 88.
3. Magill, *Masterpieces of Christian Literature* (New York: Harper & Row, 1963), p. 12.
4. Macgregor, *op. cit.*, p. 88.
5. Alexander Roberts and James Donaldson (eds.), *Ante-Nicene Fathers*, Vol. 1, (Grand Rapids, Mich.: Wm. B. Eerdman's Pub. Co., 1973), p. 254.
6. Cecil John Cadoux, *op. cit.*, p. 272; Roland H. Bainton, *Christian Attitudes Toward War and Peace* (Nashville: Abingdon Press, 1960), p. 72, quoting from Justin Martyr, First Apology, chap. 39.
7. Cadoux, *op. cit.*, p. 272; see also Arthur and Lila Weinburg (eds.), *Instead of Violence* (Boston: Beacon Press, 1968), p. 445; James O'Gara, *The Church and War* (Washington, D.C.: National Council of Catholic Men, 1967), p. 10.
8. Macgregor, *op. cit.*, p. 83; Weinberg, *op. cit.*, p. 445.
9. Bainton, *op. cit.*, p. 71.
10. Cadoux, *op. cit.*, p. 258.
11. Lake (ed.), *op. cit.*, p. 135.
12. Bainton, *op. cit.*, pp. 77, 78.
13. Cadoux, *op. cit.*, p. 256, 264; O'Gara, *op. cit.*, p. 11.
14. Roberts and Donaldson, *op. cit.*, Vol. 2, p. 147.
15. Stanley Windass, *Christianity Versus Violence* (London: Sheed and Ward, 1964), p. 8.
16. *Ibid.*, p. 7. See also Macgregor, *op. cit.*, p. 88.
17. O'Gara, *op. cit.*, p. 11.
18. Cadoux, *op. cit.*, p. 403.
19. Bainton, *op. cit.*, pp. 72, 77.
20. William Jurgens, *The Faith of the Early Fathers* (Collegeville, Minn.: Liturgical Press, 1970), p. 92.
21. *Ibid.*, p. 105.
22. Cadoux, *op. cit.*, p. 423.
23. Windass, *op. cit.*, p. 1.
24. Roberts and Donaldson, *op. cit.*, Vol. 3, p. 99.
25. *Ibid.*, p. 73.
26. *Ibid.*, p. 331.
27. Beckwith, *The Book of Peace* (Philadelphia: Perkins & Purves, 1945), p. 184.
28. Weinberg, *op. cit.*, p. 452.
29. Macgregor, *op. cit.*, p. 89.

30. Bainton, *op. cit.*, p. 70.
31. *Ibid.*, p. 73. See also Cadoux, *op. cit.*, p. 404. Compare "Top Commander in Vietnam Joins Church," *Catholic Herald Citizen* (Milwaukee, Wis.: December 26, 1970).
32. Roberts and Donaldson, *op. cit.*, Vol. 13, p. 45. But in the same writing he states that "we follow the professions of sailor, soldier, planter, merchant, we put at your service our labour and our industry." In another translation the meaning is changed. "We sail with you, and fight with you" may not specifically mean "we follow the professions of sailor, soldier," etc. See Alexander Roberts and James Donaldson (eds.), *The Ante-Nicene Fathers*, Vol. 3 (Grand Rapids, Mich.: Wm. B. Eerdman's Pub. Co., 1973).
33. Roberts and Donaldson, *op. cit.*, Vol. 3, p. 99.
34. Beckwith, *op. cit.*, p. 182.
35. Cadoux, *op. cit.*, p. 121.
36. Windass, *op. cit.*, p. 12.
37. Gordon Zahn (ed.), *Thomas Merton on Peace* (New York: McCall Pub. Co., 1971), p. 41.
38. Albert Marrin, *op. cit.*, p. 30.
39. Macgregor, *op. cit.*, p. 88.
40. Merton, *op. cit.*, p. 42.
41. Cadoux, *op. cit.*, p. 424.
42. Windass, *op. cit.*, p. 12, 13.
43. Jacques Ellul, *Violence* (New York: Seabury Press, 1969), p. 11.
44. Bainton, *op. cit.*, p. 78.
45. P. 88; see also Cadoux, *op. cit.*, p. 403, 404.
46. Bainton, *op. cit.*, p. 73, 78; Cadoux, *op. cit.*, p. 424.
47. Macgregor, *op. cit.*, p. 89.
48. O'Gara, *op. cit.*, p. 11.
49. Roberts and Donaldson, *op. cit.*, Vol. 5, p. 432.
50. Bainton, *op. cit.*, p. 73.
51. *Ibid.*, p. 73.
52. Windass, *op. cit.*, p. 13.
53. Weinberg, *op. cit.*, p. 450.
54. See Marrin, *op. cit.*, pp. 40-42; Ellul, *op. cit.*, p. 10; Bainton, *op. cit.*, p. 70.
55. O'Gara, *op. cit.*, p. 11, 12.
56. *Ibid.*
57. Roberts and Donaldson, *op. cit.*, Vol. 6, p. 415.
58. Pope John XXIII, *op. cit.*, par. 14.
59. Windass, *op. cit.*, p. 8, 9.
60. Weinberg, *op. cit.*, p. 445.
61. O'Gara, *op. cit.*, p. 12. See also Ellul, *op. cit.*, p. 10; Bainton, *op. cit.*, p. 78; and Cadoux, *op. cit.*, p. 565.
62. Macgregor, *op. cit.*, p. 89.
63. Weinberg, *op. cit.*, p. 449; also Ellul, *op. cit.*, p. 11.
64. *Ibid.*, p. 448.
65. Beckwith, *op. cit.*, p. 64.
66. Marrin, *op. cit.*, p. 19.
67. Beckwith, *op. cit.*, p. 183, 184; Cadoux, *op. cit.*, p. 590.
68. Beckwith, *op. cit.*, p. 184; Cadoux, *op. cit.*, p. 574.

69. Beckwith, *op. cit.*, p. 188; Cadoux, *op. cit.*, p. 577.
70. Beckwith, *op. cit.*, pp. 185-188.
71. *Ibid.*, pp. 191-192.
72. Windass, *op. cit.*, p. 9.
73. Bainton, *op. cit.*, p. 73.
74. Windass, *op. cit.*, p. 10.
75. *Ibid.*, p. 14.
76. *Ibid.*, p. 15.
77. *Ibid.*, p. 17.
78. Cadoux, *op. cit.*, pp. 430, 433.
79. *Ibid.*, p. 362.
80. *Ibid.*, p. 591.
81. Canon 3, *First Council of Arles* (Provence, France, AD 314).
82. *The Law of Love and the Law of Violence* (New York: Holt, Rinehart & Winston, 1971), pp. 52, 53.
83. *Ibid.*
84. Cadoux, *op. cit.*, p. 589.
85. William A. Jurgens, *op. cit.*, p. 326.
86. *Ibid.*, p. 404.
87. Germain Grisez, *Abortion: The Myths, the Realities, and the Arguments* (New York: Corpus Books, 1970), pp. 130, 140.

Chapter Six

1. Frederick Copleston, *A History of Philosophy* (New York: Image, 1963). See also Lebreton and Zeiller, *Emergence of the Church in the Roman World* (New York: Collier Books, 1962).
2. Macgregor, *op. cit.*, p. 90.
3. O'Gara, *op. cit.*, p. 18. Augustine's just-war theory was adopted from the Roman Cicero and is not basically Christian, Marrin, *op. cit.*, pp. 49-53.
4. Windass, *op. cit.*, p. 23.
5. O'Gara, *op. cit.*, p. 19.
6. Marrin, *op. cit.*, p. 61.
7. Cadoux, *op. cit.*, p. 432.
8. *Ibid.*, p. 30.
9. *Ibid.*, pp. 43-45.
10. *Ibid.*, p. 65.
11. *Ibid.*, p. 66. Augustine's teaching is simply Old Testament. See Germain Grisez. *Abortion: The Myths, the Realities, and the Arguments* (New York: Corpus Books, 1970), pp. 147, 148.
12. Augustine, translated by Marcus Dods, *The City of God* (New York: Modern Library, 1950), p. 683.
13. *Ibid.*, p. 687.
14. *Ibid.*, p. 686.
15. O'Gara, *op. cit.*, p. 19.
16. Windass, *op. cit.*, p. 27.
17. Augustine, *op. cit.*, ix.
18. Windass, *op. cit.*, p. 32. Augustine condemns abortion but authorizes war. See Grisez, *op. cit.*, pp. 147, 148.
19. O'Gara, *op. cit.*, p. 25.

20. Marrin, *op. cit.*, pp. 69-71. Aquinas condemns abortion but authorizes war. See Grisez. pp. 321-326.
21. Ellul, *op. cit.*, p. 12. See also Michael DeBedoyere, *Francis* (New York: Image, 1962), on pp. 171-185 for an account of St. Francis and nonviolence.
22. John Moorman, *A History of the Franciscan Order* (London: Oxford University Press, 1968), p. 13.
23. *Ibid.*, p. 226.
24. *Ibid.*, p. 192.
25. O'Gara, *op. cit.*, p. 29.
26. Marrin, *op. cit.*, pp. 158-160.
27. Windass, *op. cit.*, p. 100.
28. Heinrich Bornkamm, *Luther's Doctrine of the Two Kingdoms* (Philadelphia: Fortress, 1966), p. 9. (The author is indebted for notes 29 through 31 to Charles A. Brophy, a Lutheran seminarian, for his study entitled "Martin Luther's Attitudes Toward Violence and Non-Violence" (unpublished), Lutheran Theological Seminary, 1971.)
29. "Temporal Authority: to What Extent It Should Be Obeyed," *Luther's Works* (St. Louis: Concordia, 1959), Vol. 45, p. 101.
30. "An Open Letter on the Harsh Book Against the Peasants," *Luther's Works* (St. Louis: Concordia, 1959), Vol. 46, p. 49.
31. "Temporal Authority," *op. cit.*, p. 124.
32. Erik Erikson, *Young Man Luther* (New York: W. W. Norton & Co., Inc., 1962), p. 238.
33. *Ibid.*, p. 235.
34. John Calvin, *On God and Political Duty*, John T. McNeill (ed.), (New York: The Liberal Arts Press, 1956), p. 70.
35. *Ibid.*, p. 59-61.

Chapter Seven

1. J. Messner, *Social Ethics* (St. Louis; B. Herder Book Co., 1952), p. 642.
2. *Ibid.*, p. 646, 647.
3. See Richard McSorley, *Kill for Peace?* (New York: Corpus Papers, 1970), pp. 31-41.
4. Merton, *op. cit.*, p. 123.
5. Bainton, *op. cit.*, p. 234.
6. Bertrand L. Conway, *The Question Box* (New York: Paulist Press, 1929), iv.
7. *Ibid.*, p. 427.
8. *Ibid.*
9. *Ibid.*
10. Corbett, Fitsimons & Smith (eds.), *World History, The Catholic High School Social Studies Series* (New York: W. H. Sadlier, 1957), pp. 115, 116.
11. Meng & Gergely (eds.), *American History* (New York: W. H. Sadlier, 1954), p. 39.
12. John Sherrin (New York: Paulist Press, 1973), p. 42.
13. Adolph Hitler, translated by Ralph Manheim, *Mein Kampf* (Boston: Houghton Mifflin Co., 1943), p. 112.
14. *Ibid.*, p. 288.
15. *Ibid.*, p. 65.
16. Pope John XXIII, *Pacem in Terris* (Washington, D.C.: National Catholic Wel-

fare Conference, 1963) par. 114.
17. *Ibid.*, 182.
18. *Ibid.*, 113.
19. *Ibid.*, 158.
20. Abbott, *op. cit.*, p. 295.
21. *Ibid.*
22. McSorley, *op. cit.*, p. 34. See also Drinan, *Vietnam and Armageddon* (New York: Sheed & Ward, 1970), pp. 7-40; and Douglass, *The Non-violent Cross* (London: Macmillan, 1968), pp. 137, 182.
23. Pope John XXIII, *op. cit.*, par. 128.
24. Compare this statement with Pope Paul who follows traditional scholastic philosophy and distinguishes between offensive and defensive war.
25. Pope John XXIII, *op. cit.*, par. 113.
26. Abbott, *op. cit.*, p. 80.
27. *Ibid.*, p. 293.
28. *Ibid.*
29. McSorley, *op. cit.*, p. 37.
30. *Ibid.*, p. 37.
31. Abbott, *op. cit.*, p. 291.
32. *Ibid.*, p. 79.
33. Pope Paul VI, Apostolic Letter to Cardinal Maurice Roy (Washington, D.C.: Press Service, U.S. Catholic Conference, May 14, 1971), p. 1. See also *A Call to Action: Apostolic Letter on the Eightieth Anniversary of Rerum Novarum* (Washington, D.C.: U.S. Catholic Conference, 1971).
34. *Ibid.*, p. 2.
35. *Ibid.*, p. 9.
36. *Ibid.*, p. 10.
37. *Ibid.*, p. 10.
38. *Ibid.*, p. 11.
39. *Ibid.*, p. 14.
40. *Ibid.*, p. 16.
41. *Ibid.*, p. 20.
42. *Justice in the World, An Exposition of Topics to Be Discussed in the Second General Session*, Typis Polygottis Vaticanis, MCMLXXI, p. 5. The document was written in May 1971. Compare the outcome of the Synod's efforts in *The Ministerial Priesthood—Justice in the World* (Washington, D.C.: National Conference of Catholic Bishops, 1972).
43. *Ibid.*, p. 11.
44. Egan, *op. cit.*, p. 67.
45. "Justice in the World," *op. cit.*, p. 12.
46. *Ibid.*, p. 14.
47. *Ibid.*, pp. 15, 16.
48. *Ibid.*, p. 16.
49. *Ibid.*, p. 22. The report talks of "her message" referring to the Catholic Church, when we should be talking of Christ's message.
50. *Ibid.*, p. 23.
51. *Ibid.*, p. 6, quoting Isaiah, chap. 42, vv. 1-4.
52. Pope Paul VI, *Apostolic Letter, op. cit.*, p. 14.
53. *Ibid.*, p. 9.

Chapter Eight

1. Priests of the Milwaukee Catholic Archdiocese stated in 1971 that "Violence in the name of peace is a contradiction in terms" (*Milwaukee Journal,* May 1971).
2. *The Ecumenist,* Vol. 9, No. 2, Jan.-Feb. 1971.
3. *Ibid.*, p. 26.
4. *Ibid.*, p. 27. An interesting contrast with Berrigan's "nonviolence" is the Mennonite approach. The Mennonites would not participate in the antiwar demonstrations of May Day 1971. After the demonstrations were over, a group of Mennonites came to Washington and cleaned up the trash and repaired broken benches and buildings. Their leader said, "You can't win by destroying. It has to be done by love." (*Washington Post,* May 22, 1971.)
5. Thomas Merton (ed.), *Gandhi on Non-Violence* (New York: New Directions, 1965), p. 39.
6. *Op. cit.*, pp. 28, 29.
7. "The Burden of the Berrigans," (*Holy Cross Quarterly,* Vol. 4, No. 1, Jan. 1971), p. 17.
8. *Fellowship,* May 1971, p. 17.
9. Zahn, *Thomas Merton on Peace, op. cit.*, xxxvii.
10. *Ibid.*, p. 232.
11. Henry Bettenson, *Documents of the Christian Church* (New York: Oxford University Press, 1963), pp. 189, 190.
12. Henry Lucas, *The Renaissance and the Reformation* (New York: Harper & Bros., 1934), p. 587.
13. James A. Corbett *et al, World History* (New York: W. H. Sadlier, 1953).
14. Nino Lo Bello,\ *The Vatican Empire* (New York: Trident Press, 1968), p. 105.
15. Grisez, *op. cit.*, pp. 139, 140.
16. Zahn, Thomas Merton on Peace, *op. cit.*, p. 33. See also "Pacifism is Not Church Teaching" (Milwaukee, Wis.: *Catholic Herald Citizen,* Mar. 13, 1971).
17. *Ibid.*, p. 33.
18. *Ibid.*, p. 36.
19. *Ibid.*, p. 44.
20. *Ibid.*, xix.
21. Zahn, *German Catholics and Hitler's Wars* (New York: Dutton, 1969), p. 27. See also pp. 7, 9-11, 17,)18, 67-74, 83-102.
22. *Ibid.*, p. 125. American bishops were strong advocates of armed intervention prior to the Vietnam war (Milwaukee, Wis.: *Catholic Herald Citizen,* Sept. 26, 1970), p. 1.
23. *Ibid.*, p. 39.
24. *Ibid.*, p. 212.
25. *Thomas Merton on Peace, op. cit.*, p. 166. See A. K. Jameson, "Unarmed Against Facism." *Peace News* (London: Peace News, Ltd., 1963) for an account on non-violent resistance on the part of Norwegians including their church.
26. Jerre Mangione, *A Passion for Sicilians — The World Around Danilo Dolci* (New York: Marrow & Co., 1968), p. 140.
27. *Ibid.*, p. 322.
28. *Ibid.*, p. 347.
29. *Ibid.*, pp. 18, 61.
30. Melville Harcourt, *Portraits of Destiny* (New York: Sheed & Ward,1966), pp.82,83.

31. Paul Rosenweig (ed.), *The Wisdom of Tolstoy* (New York: Philosophical Ltd., 1968), p. 44.
32. James Finn, *Protest: Pacifism and Politics* (New York: Vintage Books, 1968), p.147.
33. *Ibid.*, p. 146, 147.
34. *Ibid.*, p. 80.
35. Gordon Zahn, *In Solitary Witness* (Boston: Beacon Press, 1964).
36. For those who would like to know more about Dorothy Day see her books *Loaves and Fishes* (New York: Harper & Row, 1963) and *The Long Loneliness* (New York: Harper & Row, 1952). Also see William D. Miller, *A Harsh and Dreadful Love* (New York: Doubleday, 1974).
37. Peter Matthiessen, *Sal Si Puedes: Cesar Chavez and the New American Revolution* (New York: Random House, 1969), pp. 195, 196.
38. For those who would like to know more about Mother Teresa see Malcolm Muggeridge *Something Beautiful for God* (New York: Harper & Row, 1969).
39. For those who would like to know more about Dom Helder Camera, see Dom Helder Camera, *Spiral of Violence* (Denville, N.J.: Dimension Books, 1970); and Jose de Boucker, *Dom Helder Camera: The Violence of a Peacemaker* (New York: Orbis Books, 1970).
40. Finn, *op. cit.*, pp. 45, 52, 53.
41. Richard McSorley, *Kill for Peace?* (New York: Corpus Papers, 1970).
42. Leonard Weber, *Christianity and War* (Beverly Hills, Calif.: Bruce, 1972), p. 97.
43. *Ibid.*
44. See Reinhold Niebuhr, "Why the Christian Church Is Not Pacifist," *Christianity and Power Politics* (New York: Charles Scribner's Sons, 1940); and Paul Ramsey, *The Just War: Force and Political Responsibility* (New York: Charles Scribner's Sons, 1968).
45. Macgregor, *op. cit.*, p. 117.
46. *Ibid.*, p. 118; see MacGregor generally for a Protestant pacifist theology and Brock, *op. cit.*, generally for a history of the American historic peace church movement.
47. "Justice in the World," *op. cit.*, p. 25.

Chapter Nine

1. See Thomas Merton (ed.), *Gandhi on Non-Violence, op. cit.*, pp. 26, 34.
2. Lerone Bennet, *What Manner of Man* (Chicago: Johnson Pub., Co., Inc., 1964), pp. 65, 66.
3. Coretta Scott King, *My Life with Martin Luther King, Jr.* (New York: Avon, 1967), p. 141.
4. William R. Miller, *Martin Luther King, Jr.* (New York: Weybright & Talley, 1968), p. 227.
5. Martin Luther King, Jr., *Strength to Love* (New York: Harper & Row, 1963), pp. 46, 47.
6. *Ibid.*, p. 49.
7. Martin Luther King, Jr. *Why We Can't Wait* (New York: Signet, 1964), pp. 63, 64.
8. Coretta Scott King, *op. cit.*, pp. 316, 317.
9. Graham and Gurr (ed.), *Violence in America* (New York: Signet, 1969), pp. 184, 187.

10. McSorley, *op. cit.*, p. 20.
11. Windass, *op. cit.*, p. 42.
12. Bainton, *op. cit.*, pp. 99-100.
13. *Ibid.*, p. 132.
14. *Ibid.*, p. 133.
15. *Ibid.*, pp. 203, 204.
16. Ellul, *op. cit.*, p. 102.
17. Graham and Gurr, *op. cit.*, p. 61.
18. Dee Brown, *Bury My Heart at Wounded Knee* (New York: Bantam, 1972), pp. 1, 2. See also Vine Deloria, *Custer Died for My Sins* (London: Macmillan, 1967). for another good book on violence toward Indians.
19. Jack Anderson, "Washington Merry-Go-Round" (Washington, D.C.: *Washington Post,* Feb. 25, 1971).
20. Graham and Gurr, *op. cit.*, p. 44.
21. *Ibid.*, p. 45.
22. *Ibid.*, p. 59.
23. Adin Ballou, *Christian Non-Resistance* (Philadelphia: Universal Peace Union, 1910), p. 193.
24. *Ibid.*, p. 156.
25. *Ibid.*, p. 170.
26. *Ibid.*, p. 158.
27. *Ibid.*, p. 165.
28. Bainton, *op. cit.*, p. 266.
29. *Ibid.*
30. Douglass, *op. cit.*, p. 279.
31. *Ibid.*
32. Peter Brock, *Pacifism in the United States* (Princeton, N.J.: Princeton Univ. Press, 1968), p. 3.
33. *Ibid.*, p. 36.
34. *Ibid.*, p. 60.
35. Abraham Maslow (ed.), *New Knowledge in Human Values* (Chicago: Henry Regnery, 1970).
36. Richard Gregg, *The Power of Non-Violence* (New York: Schocken, 1969).
37. Jurgens, *op. cit.*, p. 115.

Selected Bibliography

Books and Pamphlets

Abbott, William M. (ed.). *Documents of Vatican II*. New York: Guild Press, 1966.
Augustine. *The City of God*. New York: Modern Library, 1950.
Bainton, Roland H. *Christian Attitudes Toward War and Peace*. Nashville: Abingdon Press, 1960.
Ballou, Adin. *Christian Non-Resistance*. Philadelphia: Universal Peace Union, 1910.
Beckwith, George. *The Book of Peace*. Philadelphia: Perkins and Purves Pub Co., 1845.
Bettenson, Henry. *Documents of the Christian Church*. New York: Oxford University Press, 1947.
Bornkamm, Heinrich. *Luther's Doctrine of the Two Kingdoms*. Philadelphia: Fortress, 1966.
Brock, Peter. *Pacifism in the United States*. Princeton, N.J.: Princeton University Press, 1968.
Brown, Dee. *Bury My Heart at Wounded Knee*. New York: Bantam, 1972.
Cadoux, Cecil John. *The Early Church and the World*. Edinburgh, Scotland: Clark Pub. Co., 1925.
————. *The Early Christian Attitude to War*. London: Headley Bros., 1919.
Copleston, Frederick. *A History of Philosophy*. New York: Image, 1963.
Cramer, Raymond L. *The Psychology of Jesus and Mental Health*. Grand Rapids, Mich.: Zondervan Pub. House, 1959.
Cullmann, Oscar, *Jesus and the Revolutionaries*. New York: Harper & Row, 1970.
Day, Dorothy. *The Long Loneliness*. New York: Harper & Row, 1952.
————. *Loaves and Fishes*. New York: Harper & Row, 1963.
DeBedoyere, Michael. *Francis*. New York: Image, 1962.
Deloria, Vine. *Custer Died for My Sins*. London: Macmillan, 1967.
Dolan, John P. (ed.). *The Essential Erasmus*. New York: Mentor, 1964.
Douglass, James. *The Non-Violent Cross*. London: Macmillan, 1968.
Drinan, James. *Vietnam and Armageddon*. New York: Sheed & Ward, 1970.
Egan, Eileen (ed.). *The War That Is Forbidden: Peace Beyond Vatican II*. American Pax Association, no date.
Eller, Vernard. *King Jesus' Manual of Arms for the 'Armless*. Nashville: Abingdon Press, 1973.
Ellul, Jacques. *Violence*. New York: Seabury Press, 1969.
Fast, Henry. *Jesus and Human Conflict*. Scottdale, Pa.: Herald Press, 1959.
Gandhi, M. K. *Non-Violent Resistance*. New York: Schocken, 1970.
Graham and Gurr (ed.). *Violence in America*. New York: Signet, 1969.
Gregg, Richard. *The Power of Non-Violence*. New York: Fellowship Publications, 1951.

Griesez, Germain. *Abortion: The Myths, the Realities, and the Arguments.* New York: Corpus Books, 1970.
Guinan, Edward (ed.). *Peace and Non-Violence.* New York: Paulist Press, 1973.
Harcourt, Melville. *Portraits of Destiny.* New York: Sheed & Ward, 1966.
Hershberger, Guy. *War, Peace, and Nonresistance.* Scottdale, Pa.: Herald Press, 1953.
Holy Bible. (*The Jerusalem Bible*, edited by Alexander Jones. New York: Doubleday, 1966. *The New English Bible*, New York: Cambridge University Press, 1961, 1970. *The Common Bible*, Revised Standard Version. New York: Collins, 1973.)
Jepson, John J. *St. Augustine: The Lord's Sermon on the Mount.* Westminster, Md.: Newman Press, 1956.
King, Martin Luther. *Strength to Love.* New York: Pocket Books, 1968.
Lake, Kirsopp. (ed.). *The Apostolic Fathers.* London: Harvard University Press, 1970.
Lasserre, Jean. *War and the Gospel.* Scottdale, Pa.: Herald Press, 1962.
Lo Bello, Nino. *The Vatican Empire.* New York: Trident Press, 1968.
MacGregor, G. H. C. *The New Testament Basis of Pacifism.* New York: Fellowship Pub., 1954.
Mangione, Jerre. *A Passion for Sicilians: The World Around Danilo Dolci.* New York: Morrow & Co., 1968.
Marrin, Albert (ed.). *War and the Christian Conscience.* Chicago: Henry Regnery Co., 1971.
Matthiessen, Peter. *Sal Si Puedes: Cesar Chavez and the New American Revolution.* New York: Random House, 1969.
McNeill, John T. (ed.). *John Calvin on God and Political Duty.* New York: Liberal Arts Press, 1956.
McSorley, Richard. *Kill for Peace?* New York: Corpus Papers, 1970.
Merton, Thomas. *Faith and Violence.* Notre Dame: University of Notre Dame Press, 1968.
———— (ed.). *Gandhi on Non-Violence.* New York: New Directions, 1965.
Lloyd-Jones, D. Martyn. *Studies in the Sermon on the Mount* (Vol. 1). Gross Point, Mich.: Willard B. Eerdman's Pub. Co., 1967.
Miller, William R. *Martin Luther King, Jr.* New York: Weybright and Talley, 1968.
Muggeridge, Malcolm. *Something Beautiful for God, Mother Teresa of Calcutta.* New York: Harper & Row, 1971.
Niebuhr, Reinhold. *Christianity and Power Politics.* New York: Charles Scribner's Sons, 1940.
O'Gara, James. *The Church and War.* Washington, D.C.: National Council of Catholic Men, 1967.
Pope John XXIII. *Pacem in Terris.* Washington, D.C.: National Catholic Welfare Conference, 1963.
Pope Paul VI. *Apostolic Letter to Cardinal Maurice Roy.* Washington, D.C.: United States Catholic Conference, 1971.
Ramsey, Paul. *The Just War: Force and Political Responsibility.* New York: Charles Scribner's Sons, 1968.
Rosenweig, Paul (ed.). *The Wisdom of Tolstoy.* New York Philosophical Library, 1968.
Ross, James (ed.). *The War Within.* New York: Sheed & Ward, 1971.
Rutenber, Culbert. *The Dagger and the Cross.* Nyack: Fellowship Pub., 1958.

Shaffer, Jerome A. (ed.). *Violence*. New York: David McKay Co., Inc., 1971.
Slack, Kenneth. *Martin Luther King*. London: SCM Press Ltd., 1970.
Tolstoy, Leo. *The Law of Love and the Law of Violence*. New York: Holt, Rinehart and Winston, 1971.
————. *A Confession, the Gospel in Brief and What I Believe*. London: Oxford University Press, 1967.
————. *On Civil Disobedience and Non-Violence*. New York: Signet, 1967.
————. *The Kingdom of God Is Within You*. New York: Noonday Press, 1970.
Twain, Mark. *The War Prayer*. New York: Harper Colophon, 1970.
Weber, Leonard. *Christianity and War*. Beverly Hills, Calif.: Bruce, 1972.
Weinberg, Arthur and Lila. *Instead of Violence*. Boston: Beacon Press, 1968.
Windass, Stanley. *Christianity Versus Violence*. London: Sheed & Ward, 1964.
Windisch, Stanley. *The Meaning of the Sermon on the Mount*. Philadelphia: Westminister Press, 1950.
Yoder, John H. *Nevertheless, A Meditation on the Varieties and Shortcomings of Religious Pacifism*. Scottdale, Pa.: Herald Press, 1971.
————. *The Politics of Jesus*. Grand Rapids, Mich.: William B. Eerdman's Pub. Co., 1972.
Zahn, Gordon. *German Catholics and Hitler's Wars*. New York: Dutton, 1965.
————. *In Solitary Witness*. Boston: Beacon Press, 1964.
————. (ed.). *Thomas Merton on Peace*. New York: McCall Pub. Co., 197.

Periodicals

Day, Dorothy, "The Berrigans and Property Rights," *Fellowship Magazine* (May 1971), p. 25.
Jameson, A. K., "Unarmed Against Facism," *Peace News* (London: Peace News Ltd., Apr. 1963).
"Letter from Fr. Daniel Berrigan to the Weathermen," *The Ecumenist* (Vol. 9, No. 1, Nov.-Dec. 1970/Jan.-Feb. 1971), pp. 25-29.
"The Burden of the Berrigans," *Holy Cross Quarterly* (Vol. 4, No. 1, Jan. 1971).

Index

William R. Durland is chairman of the Department of Philosophy and Religion at Purdue University in Fort Wayne, Indiana. Born on March 28, 1931, in New York City, he is married to Leona M. Durland. They have three children, Patrick 16, Michael 14, and Jenifer 8.

Professor Durland holds an AB in political science and history from Bucknell University, and a Doctor of Jurisprudence degree from Georgetown University Law Center. He has been admitted to the practice of law in Virginia, Wisconsin, Indiana, and District of Columbia, and before the Supreme Court of the United States. He is currently doing graduate study in theology at the University of Notre Dame.

He has taught courses on the subject of violence and nonviolence at St. Paul's College of Catholic University, for the University of Virginia, at Georgetown University, and at Notre Dame, as well as Purdue.

A former member of the Virginia state legislature (specializing in the fields of poverty, conservation, consumer affairs, mental health, and retardation), he helped to found the Community for Creative Non-Violence in Washington, D.C., and the Center for Peace Studies at Georgetown University. He is the director of the Center for the Study of the Person at Purdue University at Fort Wayne.

Dr. Durland's published articles include "The Bishop of Prato and American Law" in the *Georgetown Law Journal* and "Violence and Virginia" in the *Virginia Sentinel*. With Dr. William Bruening, he is the coeditor of an anthology entitled *Ethical Issues: A Search for Patterns in the Contemporary Conscience*, which includes two essays by him: "The Moral Equivalent of Violence" and "Four Theories of Law and Morality."

WHEN?

By Emily Sargent Councilman

The Herods of this world,
fearful for their power,
send soldiers
to slaughter
innocents.
The Caesars of the earth
dispatch armies
to implement decrees
for conquest
and taxes.

But the God
above all governors
came, Himself.
His armor and His purpose:
love. . . .
We have read the pages
of centuries.
When will we *dare*
to write
peace?